A. C. Croft, APR

Managing a Public Relations Firm for Growth and Profit

Pre-publication REVIEWS, COMMENTARIES, EVALUATIONS . . .

"**C**roft's book is the public relations equivalent of the *Physician's Desk Reference*. It should be on the desk of the principal or top executive of every public relations firm.

If you're starting your own business, read the entire book. Then, reread it every six months. Each time you read the 'Croft Manual' you'll be less apprehensive and more comforted and appreciative.

It is amazing that many successful public relations people are do-it-yourselfers who learn on the job. I wish that I had this book when I operated a public relations firm. It would have reduced the stress and increased the profits, even if I didn't do everything the 'Croft Way.'"

Richard Weiner, MS
*Public Relations Consultant,
New York City*

"**T**his book is vintage Al Croft from cover to cover. Al never minces words. He's always straightforward and direct—and always willing to share his tremendous store of knowledge about public relations business.

In his one-on-one counsel and in this book, Al is always enthusiastic about the public relations business. He projects that enthusiasm, inspiring others to be 'exceptional.' As Al states in this great book, 'Exceptional has to be the least acceptable standard . . . without exception.' If I were to start all over again, this is the book I would want on my desk at all times. I can't even begin to imagine how much time it would have saved me in those early years of entrepreneurship."

Sara Jean Thoms, BS, MIM
J. Thoms & Associates, Inc.,
Minneapolis, Minnesota

"**W**hen it comes to PR agency management, A. C. Croft has been there, done that—and he knows how to teach the way. There's not a better agency doctor on the scene today, and this new book distills his knowledge into what will become the field's classic 'how-to' manual.

Croft has a unique grasp of what makes an agency tick. *Managing a Public Relations Firm for Growth and Profit* reflects his special gift for simplifying the process, and for focusing on the fundamentals that produce agency growth and profit.

This is not a pompous book. Don't expect to find lofty theories or grand concepts. Do expect to learn what works and what doesn't. Do look to it for specific, concrete steps to help you promote your firm better, win more business, forecast income, and stay profitable in good times and bad. Do turn to it for sound advice from the best systems person in the business.

Three words sum up this new book: practical, readable, and valuable. Agency practitioner or client, you will come away from it with dozens of ideas to make your everyday work more organized and more productive. And if you're in agency management, it's a goldmine of counsel you won't find in anything else published to date."

W. Ward White, PhD, APR
Vice President, Communications,
Northwestern Mutual Life

The Haworth Press, Inc.

Managing a Public Relations Firm for Growth and Profit

HAWORTH Marketing Resources
Innovations in Practice & Professional Services
William J. Winston, Senior Editor

New, Recent, and Forthcoming Titles:

Cases and Select Readings in Health Care Marketing edited by Robert E. Sweeney, Robert L. Berl, and William J. Winston

Marketing Planning Guide by Robert E. Stevens, David L. Loudon, and William E. Warren

Marketing for Churches and Ministries by Robert E. Stevens and David L. Loudon

The Clinician's Guide to Managed Mental Health Care by Norman Winegar

Framework for Market-Based Hospital Pricing Decisions by Shahram Heshmat

Professional Services Marketing: Strategy and Tactics by F. G. Crane

A Guide to Preparing Cost-Effective Press Releases by Robert H. Loeffler

How to Create Interest-Evoking, Sales-Inducing, Non-Irritating Advertising by Walter Weir

Market Analysis: Assessing Your Business Opportunities by Robert E. Stevens, Philip K. Sherwood, and J. Paul Dunn

Selling Without Confrontation by Jack Greening

Persuasive Advertising for Entrepreneurs and Small Business Owners: How to Create More Effective Sales Messages by Jay P. Granat

Marketing Mental Health Services to Managed Care by Norman Winegar and John L. Bistline

New Product Screening: A Step-Wise Approach by William C. Lesch and David Rupert

Church and Ministry Strategic Planning: From Concept to Success by R. Henry Migliore, Robert E. Stevens, and David L. Loudon

Business in Mexico: Managerial Behavior, Protocol, and Etiquette by Candace Bancroft McKinniss and Arthur A. Natella

Managed Service Restructuring in Health Care–A Strategic Approach in a Competitive Environment by Robert L. Goldman and Sanjib K. Mukherjee

A Marketing Approach to Physician Recruitment by James Hacker, Don C. Dodson, and M. Thane Forthman

Marketing for CPAs, Accountants, and Tax Professionals edited by William J. Winston

Strategic Planning for Not-for-Profit Organizations by R. Henry Migliore, Robert E. Stevens, and David L. Loudon

Marketing Planning in a Total Quality Environment by Robert E. Linneman and John L. Stanton, Jr.

Managing Sales Professionals: The Reality of Profitability by Joseph P. Vaccaro

Publicity for Mental Health Clinicians: Using TV, Radio, and Print Media to Enhance Your Public Image by Douglas H. Ruben

Squeezing a New Service into a Crowded Market by Dennis J. Cahill

Managing a Public Relations Firm for Growth and Profit by A. C. Croft

Managing a Public Relations Firm for Growth and Profit

A. C. Croft, APR

The Haworth Press
New York • London

The Haworth Press, Inc., 10 Alice Street, Binghamton, NY 13904-1580

Paperback edition published in 1997.

Cover design by Monica L. Seifert.

Library of Congress Cataloging-in-Publication Data

Croft, A. C.
    Managing a public relations firm for growth and profit / A. C. Croft.
        p.   cm.
    Includes index.
    ISBN 0-7890-0130-6 (alk. paper)
    1. Public relations firms–Management. I. Title.
HD59.C755   1995
659.2′068–dc20   95-6818
                                                                                    CIP

CONTENTS

APPENDIXES

ABOUT THE AUTHOR

A. C. (Al) Croft, APR, is a public relations management consultant specializing in training, evaluation, and critical and conceptual thinking. He provides planning, evaluation, and counseling services to small, midsize, and national public relations firms. Mr. Croft has more than 25 years experience in national public relations firms, including 15 years in senior management, and formed his management consulting practice in 1987. Formerly, he was senior vice president and Midwest general manager of Bozell Public Relations, one of the country's largest public relations firms.

A widely published author, Mr. Croft has written for such publications as *Bank Marketing, Marketing Week, Public Relations Journal, communications briefings,* and *Advertising Age.* In addition, he is contributing editor of *Public Relations Quarterly,* for which he writes a column on public relations firm management, and editor of *Management Strategies,* a monthly subscription newsletter for public relations firm principals.

Mr. Croft conducts in-house account management seminars for public relations firms and is host and moderator of the *Sedona Round Table,* a two-day workshop for 20 noncompetitive firms held each fall in Sedona, Arizona. The Public Relations Society of America has awarded Mr. Croft two Silver Anvils, the highest recognition in the public relations profession.

Foreword

Some have thought of public relations as a craft. Others have viewed it as a profession. Still others define PR as applied social science. Al Croft looks at public relations as a service of value and as a business. And nobody knows more than Al about the business of public relations.

Like most of his peers, he was thrust into the business of managing a public relations firm. But unlike some of us who were dragged kicking and screaming from "doing PR" to running a business, Al made it his business to master the principles of good management and apply them to public relations.

In this book, he shares his wealth of knowledge about public relations management, drawing on his long experience running successful public relations operations.

To achieve success in running a public relations business, managers must satisfy the sometimes contradictory needs of at least three diverse audiences. They must provide exemplary service to clients. They must provide expansive career opportunities to employees. And they must return a reasonable profit to the guy who owns the place.

Public relations entrepreneurs are a funny lot. While owners of other kinds of businesses are unabashedly in it for all they can take out of it, your typical PR firm owner often has been satisfied by the freedom to run his own business, often substituting psychic income for dollars and cents. He or she is genuinely turned on by doing good work and getting results for clients. All too often, they have been more motivated by the thrill of winning new business and the satisfaction of serving important clients than by enhancing their firm's bottom line.

I have worked for PR firms that performed excellent work for prestigious companies for years despite the fact that these accounts were marginally, if at all, profitable. The rationale was that these clients were a ticket to attracting new clients, wear and tear on staff and the absence of profit notwithstanding.

It's no wonder that employees of PR firms that overservice and undercharge clients for their work complain that they are over-worked and underpaid. You cannot build a ball club with stressed-out players. An agency needs a staff motivated by the opportunities to share the goodies as well as the fun. The boss who may think he can do it all now, can't continue to be a one-man band as the firm grows.

The times are changing. The renewed emphasis their clients are placing on doing what it takes to maximize profits isn't lost on PR firms. Many formerly independent PR shops are now owned by other entities such as advertising agencies, holding companies and larger PR firms. Their casual ways of doing business have given way to strict adherence to the systems and processes imposed by their new parents. They find themselves valued as much or more for their contributions to the P&L than the quality of their work. It's a rude shock for former paternalistic owners to learn just how serious the new owners are about their volume and earnings expectations. Many of the old owners have found it uncomfortable to operate under a new order and have been replaced by professional managers who are accustomed to managing the bottom line.

This new breed of entrepreneurs are more serious about the business of the business than were their predecessors. They are in business to make money and they want to see their hard work rewarded. It follows that they are doing what it takes to manage for profitable growth. Some plan to cash out at some point in time and are bent on making their firms attractive to potential buyers. Others wouldn't think of working for someone else, ever. Still, they are taking steps to generate rewards that are commensurate with their efforts.

Whatever their motivation, it's no coincidence that many of these bright young agency owners are students of Al Croft. He has worked with management of scores of agencies around the country to help them manage their business profitably and has conducted seminars for their account managers on how to manage their accounts more efficiently.

His *Management Strategies* newsletter is must reading for his owner-subscribers. His annual Sedona Round Table enables a select group of PR firm principals to learn from Al and each other. I have been privileged to be a Round Table faculty member and have come away absorbing as much as I have imparted.

Now, he has given us the ultimate "how to" book in PR firm management. I would have given anything to have a book like this when I started the public relations operation for the international giant, Foote Cone & Belding.

I had spent half a career managing accounts while somebody else managed the business. I had to learn the business of public relations from scratch, and it wasn't easy. The ad folks tried to help but their business is substantially different from public relations. Their accounting systems were based on the then-sacrosanct commission system that doesn't apply to PR. Accounts were staffed by armies of handsomely rewarded vice presidents, account directors, account supervisors, and other executives that no PR account could afford. The abundant overhead charges easily absorbed by the ad side were devastating to our business.

By trial and error, hook or crook, and an understanding management, we learned how to run a profitable business. The CEO was so impressed with our success that he started the PR acquisition craze of the 1970s. But that's another story.

If you are now running or planning to run a PR firm, I guarantee you that *Managing a PR Firm for Growth and Profit* will save untold hours of pain and misery and reinventing the wheel. Al has put together an altogether remarkable book that you will refer to time and time again.

Al covers all the bases. He happens to be a skilled communicator as well as a student of management. His book is clear, concise, easy to understand, and easy to apply. He spells it all out. How to market and manage your firm. What to do. What not to do. What kind of clients to work for and what kind to avoid. How to make money. And how to lose it.

He even provides some of the basic forms and documents you will need, such as sample letters of agreement, time sheets, budget forms, and status report forms.

Running a firm today has become much more complicated, but the computer has come to the rescue. Al tells you how to harness technology to help you track vital processes such as staff utilization, performance against projections, budget status, and cash flow.

Al doesn't limit his content to the particulars of the PR business. He offers his readers very valuable suggestions on such subjects as time management and paper management that can be shared with a spouse, a friend, or even a client in another service business.

As a reader bonus, each chapter is introduced by succinct real-world wisdom from dozens of successful chiefs of successful public relations firms.

Al has directed his book to small and midsize firms. I predict that those who apply the wisdom of the ages embodied in this book to their businesses won't be small or midsized for long.

A long time ago, I took a college course from a professor who wrote a book called *Write That Book*. I urged Al Croft to write this book because it's needed and because nobody could do it better. I think you will agree.

Thomas L. Harris, APR
Fellow PRSA

Preface

This book is aimed at helping you learn to manage a public relations firm . . . for growth and profit. It will tell you what you need to know to start a PR firm and make it GO!

Perhaps, you have already made the leap and have at least a few employees and several paying clients. You may even have been in business for a number of years and consider your firm successful.

However, occasionally, or even consistently, you may suffer a disquieting sense that, after an initial spurt of business, your firm is now sitting on dead center, gaining few new clients, or even losing business that is not being replaced. Or you may experience a nagging disenchantment with your financial rewards (compared to the hours you put in).

This book will help you correct such problems by demonstrating: (1) how to market, promote and sell your firm to attract, win and hold the kind of clients you want; and (2) how to manage your firm so that it is productive, profitable and has a long-range future.

If you are a second level agency manager or a corporate PR executive toying with the idea of firm management or ownership, you will learn how to avoid duplicating the mistakes of those who have gone before you.

Senior management of national firms who read this book will be comforted by recognizing practices, precepts and philosophies that they have espoused all their professional lives. Most of what works for the 500-employee agency works equally well for the five-man (or woman) firm.

At the beginning of each chapter, you will find a brief profile of a seasoned and successful PR firm principal. These are not chief executive officers of huge international endeavors. Rather, they each own a mid-size firm generating somewhere between $1 million and $6 million a year in fee income. (There are several thousand such firms operating in the U.S. and Canada, not to mention probably a similar number in foreign ports.) Each of the firms has grown in the image of its owner/principal.

Some of the firms are generalists, working for a variety of clients; others specialize in one or more specific market niches. Some firms are fast moving, fast growing; others are laid-back with more moderate growth. In these cases, growth should not necessarily be taken as the only mark of success, but merely as an indication of the path chosen by the principal.

You would do well to listen as the principals talk about their early mistakes and heed the advice they offer.

I should also note that I have endeavored not to be chauvinistic. I was an early and enthusiastic supporter of equal pay and equal assignments for women. However, I draw the line at constantly writing "he or she"–or something ridiculous like "personagement" to substitute for management–to demonstrate my non-chauvinism. So please understand that when I write "he," it is the literary short cut to "he and/or she."

This book is based largely on my experience over seven years as a consultant to PR firm principals, and for the 25 years before that as either an employee or principal of three medium-size and very successful PR agencies. (Although the agencies I ran were divisions or subsidiaries of large national advertising and public relations firms, I operated them independently. And sometimes suffered for that affront.)

I am indebted to two clients and friends for their willingness to read parts of this volume and tell me whether they made sense. John Charleston, Chairman of Charleston/Orwig, Hartland, WI is a former Wisconsin colleague and one of the finest public relations writers that I have ever encountered. Mike Walker, President, The Walker Agency, Scottsdale, AZ started his successful firm with his wife at their dining room table 13 years ago, after being unceremoniously relieved of his PR responsibilities at a Fortune 500 corporation. I thank them for their insight and encouragement.

I also thank Tom Harris–author, professor, Big Band addict, consultant, former Vice Chairman Golin/Harris Communications, guru and friend of 20 years–who first encouraged me to write this book.

And to my wife, Irene, who shares the responsibility for A.C. Croft and Associates, how did I ever get along before I met you 25 years ago?

If this book lights a path for you through the maze of public relations firm management, I will be pleased. My final thanks go to all those who have walked that path with no light and who have stumbled in the dark. I learned from you.

A.C. Croft
Sedona, AZ

PART I.
INTRODUCTION:
THE PR AGENCY BUSINESS

PROFILE 1

CATHY ACKERMANN, PRESIDENT, ACKERMANN PUBLIC RELATIONS AND MARKETING, KNOXVILLE, TN

After serving as director of corporate marketing for the 1982 World's Fair, Ackermann founded the area's first full-service communications firm. The agency's first year's income of $250,000 grew to $2.2 million 12 years later.

However, fast expansion during the firm's early years and a lack of administrative systems took their toll. "I was having too much fun being a practitioner and was not paying enough attention to the business side," Ackermann says. "After a couple years, we said, 'We're working too hard not to make more money.' That drove us to put systems in place.

"We tightened everything that had to do with the financial side of the business. For example, every month, I look in detail at such things as the financial statement, cash flow, gross profit, billable hours and accounts receivable. I also review with each billable person the number of hours spent and actually billed to clients as well as each person's profitability and their contribution to the agency."

Six years ago, the firm began offering fully integrated marketing communications. Ackermann calls integrated marketing communications " . . . the wave of the future because clients are looking for marketing and communications partners who understand them inside out and who can be an extension of their staff." (In addition to advertising, promotion and direct marketing, about 65 percent of the firm's business is PR.)

Chapter 1

What Is a Public Relations Firm?

If you are reading this (and I assume that you are reading it, otherwise, why are you looking at the page?), you are probably in one of two situations: (1) You are thinking about or want to become the owner or manager of a public relations firm; or (2) You are already the owner or manager of a PR firm.

If you are not already the owner/manager/principal of a firm, you are probably working either for a PR firm at some level of supervision or management or are a corporate PR executive (or were until recently working for one of these organizations). If you have experience in the agency business, most of what follows should make sense. You probably know a lot of it already. If your experience is limited to corporations or not-for-profit organizations, you are in for a real learning adventure.

True, both an agency principal and a corporate PR executive need to be consummate communication professionals and able counselors. However, beyond the professional area, their responsibilities are about as similar as a rattlesnake's bite and a lover's kiss.

Corporations are pretty much alike. (OK, so maybe some of them are different.) However, about the only standard in the agency business is that there are very few standards. Hardly any agency operates exactly like any other agency. If the agency business has one major business weakness, it is this lack of standards. If this book contributes to the establishment and acceptance of more operating standards, the author will have achieved a major goal.

The majority of the dollars in the agency business funnel into a few large national agencies. (For example, the three largest firms are each at least three times larger than the fourth largest firm.) On the other hand, there are several thousand small PR firms–with an average five to six employees–operating at various levels of success. Burson Marsteller, the largest firm in the world, had more than $192 million in annual fee income and 1700 employees according to a national directory of PR firms. The smallest firm listed in this directory had about $141,000 in fee income and one employee. (For the current listing of PR firm fee income and staff size, get an annual copy of *O'Dwyer's Directory of PR Firms*, published by J.R. O'Dwyer Company, 271 Madison Avenue, New York, NY 10016.)

Agencies measure their size–and their stature–by their "net fee income." This is the amount of revenue that a firm earns from its clients through staff time hourly charges and mark-up or commissions earned on purchased items. Sometimes, if a firm wants to look bigger than it actually is, it will report "billings." Billings are the total amount invoiced to clients by a firm including staff time, mark-ups and the cost of material or services that the agency buys on behalf of its clients and then bills back to them, usually with a mark-up added.

The 17.65 percent mark-up commonly added to out-of-pocket costs by PR firms is derived from the 15 percent commission that advertising agencies historically earn on purchased advertising space or time. Stick with me, this gets complicated. If an advertising agency is charged $100 for an ad that it has purchased on behalf of a client, it sends the client a bill for $100 but only pays the media $85–the real cost of the ad–thus earning a 15 percent commission. If a PR firm buys printing worth $85, it is actually only billed $85 by the printer. To earn the same real dollar commission, it then adds 17.65 percent of $85–$15–and sends the client a bill for $100. Remember that formula; there will be a pop quiz on Tuesday.

Just to make sure that everyone is running on the same track, let's talk about a PR firm's function and purpose. They are different and often provide a source of conflict to agency principals.

A public relations firm has only one function; to serve its clients to the best of its ability and in their best interests at all times. Sometimes, this means telling the client that he or she is wrong and refusing to do the client's bidding.

An ancient piece of PR industry lore says that public relations practitioners should go to work every day prepared to resign rather than compromise their principles or ethics on their employer's behalf.

The same wisdom holds true for public relations firms. Every company or institution has the right to have their side of the story told to, examined and judged by the public. However, no agency has the option or right to color the truth or delete facts to make the story better or shine a purer light on its client.

Agencies should be prepared to resign an attractive piece of business rather than place their integrity, credibility and reputation in harm's way.

In some cases, particularly when the article or news release describes a company's past, present, or future financial condition, the agency can be held as responsible as the client for communicating untruthful information. More than one firm has faced legal attention for wittingly or unwittingly playing with the truth. In one case, a number of years ago, the owner of a prominent Midwest firm accused of distributing misleading information about a client, was forced to resign from the Public Relations Society of America, the industry's largest professional organization, rather than face an ethics tribunal.

On the other hand, a PR firm also has only one purpose; to achieve and maintain levels of income and profit that will assure a reasonable financial return to its owners and fair and competitive compensation to its employees.

The client needs the best possible service and the agency needs the largest possible income and profit. Therein lies the potential for conflict that every agency principal will encounter sooner or later and that must be managed with a win-win approach and results. Standards of ethics, integrity and credibility must guide your actions.

"Account Management,"–the responsibility umbrella under which every agency practitioner functions–has been defined as "bringing the agency's management, professional and creative services to bear against a client's problems and opportunities so that we serve the client with maximum effectiveness while also generating maximum income and profit for the agency." No small chore!

A PR firm has only one thing to sell. Its primary product is the time that employees invest on behalf of the firm's clients. Such a system requires a great deal of faith; faith by the firm's principal that employees not only will invest the proper amount of time on the client's behalf (ideally, neither more nor less than the budget calls for) but that they have recorded that time honestly, frugally and accurately. On the other side, the client must have faith that the invoice from his agency is a fair and accurate representation of the time invested on his behalf as well as an honest accounting of the expenses and out-of-pocket purchases made by the agency on his behalf.

This emphasis on the use and value of employee time is unique to service organizations such as legal, accounting and public relations firms. The importance and relevance of time places unique responsibilities on a PR firm's professional employees. It can, if not guarded, place undue emphasis on the need for productivity and profit rather than on the need for top-notch client service and satisfaction.

The emphasis on time creates oft-strange jargon; "billability" is hard to say, but everyone in the agency business knows what it means (i.e., the ability of an individual to bill a large portion of his or her on-the-job time to clients). Practitioners' value to an agency may be judged by how "billable" they are.

A PR firm becomes profitable by (1) serving its clients well; (2) controlling its costs (salaries and overhead); and (3) charging fair, competitive hourly rates.

Historically, agencies used a simple multiple of hourly salary costs–three to four times salary costs–to set hourly rates. However, such a basic approach fails to cover modern and continually rising technology and health care costs. Today, many firms establish hourly rates–or project cost estimates or fees based on them–by using a formula that divides the sum of an individual's salary cost, a share of the firm's overhead and the desired profit percentage by the number of hours that the individual is expected to bill annually. (More on this formula later.)

IS IT A FIRM OR AN AGENCY?

There are two types of public relations firms: those that are independent–owned and managed by a single individual, a partnership or a group of individuals–and those that are a department, division or subsidiary of a national PR firm, or a conglomerate or an advertising agency.

Some PR practitioners insist that there are public relations "firms" and advertising "agencies." Many of the same souls who insist that only "firm" be used also frown on abbreviating public relations as "PR." Owners and employees commonly refer to their "agency" except in more formal situations, such as a new business presentation, when they may discuss their "firm's" capabilities and exploits. To acquire new public relations representation, corporations conduct "agency searches." However, the Public Relations Society of America insists that "firm" be used in all Society communications evidently feeling that "agency" is somehow disparaging to its members.

On the other hand, everybody understands when you say, "I've been in the agency business for X years." Nobody says, "I've been in the firm business for X years." I tend to use firm and agency interchangeably and I do not mind "PR." Use whichever term you are comfortable with and that fits the situation. Don't worry about the semantics.

ON BEING SUCCESSFUL

There are also agencies that are successful: growing and profitable. And those that are not. Being either independent or subordinate has little relationship to whether your firm is successful. However, as a member of a corporate group of firms, you may be required to carry a hefty corporate overhead cost on your books over which you will have no control but which will impact your bottom line if you manage a profit center.

On the other hand, as part of a multi-office/agency corporate family, you will have the corporate bank account as a back-up. As an independent, you will be largely on your own financially with the ever-pressing need to meet your monthly "nut" (minimum cash outlay including salaries and rent as well as all other nonrebillable out-of-pocket costs).

As a corporate entity, you will have the strength and varied resources of a large national firm available to you and your clients. As an independent, you can offer prospects fast turnaround and consistent counseling by senior personnel.

YOUR BASIC RESPONSIBILITIES

To ensure that your firm is successful (i.e., growing and profitable with a staff of highly competent professionals and a bevy of satisfied, prompt-paying clients) at a minimum you must meet the following six basic responsibilities:

1. *Listen to the voices and tides impacting on your clients.* What is the media saying? What public movements are gaining credence and momentum? What nascent trends are evident? Who is more or less important than a year ago?
2. *Report and interpret what you hear.* Will burgeoning public opinion create a problem for your client? What will be the timing, dimensions and scope of the problem? What disruptions can media comment, public opinion or popular movements create in such areas as product acceptance, employee productivity or share value?
3. *Recommend policies and programs that relate corporate and public interests.* Develop programs to soothe and solve environmental concerns while protecting the organization's bottom line. Develop training or retraining programs to meet minority or senior citizen needs, compensate for economic cut backs and/or produce upgraded skills for technology jobs.
4. *Communicate honestly and fully in anticipation of and in response to the voices and tides.* Deliver your client's messages concisely, coherently and consistently to critical audiences and markets as broadly and precisely as necessary and possible.
5. *Prove that your effort moved mountains.* With the help of benchmarks, demonstrate that your communication campaign influenced public behavior, fostered product acceptance, promulgated a new idea, calmed negative opinion, dampened a fire storm, stimulated audience reaction and reached the eyes and ears of those who control your client's life or death.
6. *Get your bills out on time.* Never let a client owe you money longer than 30 days. It's called "cash flow!" And you will need it.   .

Coupling wisdom and vision with finely tuned abilities to listen, interpret, respond, communicate and demonstrate–not to mention collect what's owed you–will generate and ensure your clients' attention and confidence. And guarantee your firm's success.

MARKETING AND MANAGING YOUR FIRM

No matter what your firm's corporate status, high quality, professional client service, obviously, is essential to success. However, you will find little discussion in these pages of client service or general public relations theory and philosophy. Dozens of other books do that most admirably. Here, we will assume the quality of your client service, and concentrate on tips, instructions, philosophies, theories, and guidance to help you market and manage your firm.

But first, what kind of person must you be to function well as the king of the hill in your agency?

PROFILE 2

SHERI BENJAMIN, PRINCIPAL, THE BENJAMIN GROUP, CAMPBELL, CA

1988: You and your husband, a non-PR corporate executive, start a PR firm. In six weeks, you have 13 employees.

Six years and two children later, you run a $3 million high tech firm with 32 employees and two California offices. You have 12 healthy clients such as Toshiba and Seiko. Your entrepreneur husband, now a business consultant, spends one day a week in the office handling finances.

You offer innovative employee relations practices. To attract talented professional working mothers, your firm has benefits such as job sharing and a corporate day care center. In order to have an outdoor play area for the day care center, you buy your own building. (Husband Steve insists it was for tax purposes, but you know better.)

Your success rides on a good blend of strategic and tactical skills and strong technical specialties. You've learned that your employees need not all be like you. But if you were starting a firm today, you wouldn't do it the same way because of the lack of separation between home and business. In addition to your financial expert husband, you'd find a professional partner so you could take an unencumbered vacation.

"Decide what you want and grow the firm to that size. Don't let it get away from you. If you're still in it, you must love it," Benjamin says.

Chapter 2

What Is an Agency Principal?

Individuals who lead PR firms may be the owner, manager, partner, managing partner, president, chairman, director, general manager or some other semantic differentiation. However titled, they are *the principal*, the "first in rank, authority and importance," according to my dictionary. Thereby, instead of strewing personal titles haphazardly through these pages, we will simply refer to all firm leaders as principals.

In addition to a title, a larger office than anyone else, perhaps a leased car and other perks, what is an agency principal? To manage a successful public relations firm–independent agency, division or local office of a larger firm–you, the agency principal, need both entrepreneurial and professional strengths and skills as well as marketing and management interest and ability. You (and your staff members) must be able to skillfully and positively manage the potential conflict between your clients' need for the best-possible service and your firm's need for the most-possible income and profits.

To manage these dual responsibilities, you may need to choose between being an account executive or an agency manager; i.e., do the work or manage it. This can be a tough choice, particularly if you favor hands-on client work over administrative chores and have convinced yourself that you must focus 100 percent of your time and attention on client service. This could be a mistake!

Certainly, clients need and want access to senior practitioners for planning and counsel. They bristle when agency principals are featured in a new business presentation and then are replaced by junior professionals in day-to-day service.

In small agencies, the principal may not enjoy the luxury of back-up senior professionals. You may need to be very active in client contact and program implementation. Complicating matters is the fact that many principals enjoy the creative and professional challenges of account work and find it difficult to step aside.

It can also be comforting to ignore management problems such as slow cash flow, client or staff defections and other business disasters by staying immersed in direct client work. (The old "head in the sand" trick.) Entrepreneurs in general are not particularly well known for down-to-earth business acumen and management skills. Witness the well-documented cases of corporate entrepreneurs who have founded high visibility companies only to be forced out as the company grows because of their lack of sound management skills. These same weaknesses often cause problems for PR firms.

However, neglecting the administrative and management needs of your agency is as dangerous as neglecting your clients' needs. Further, the more your firm grows, the more your attention must be directed toward managing the business. The truth is, " The business of the business is as important as serving the client," says Cathy Ackermann, President, Ackermann Public Relations and Marketing, a thriving Knoxville, TN firm.

PROFESSIONAL EXPERIENCE AND SKILLS

What kind of experience do you need to own or manage a successful PR firm? Let's begin with the obvious. Most individuals who start their own PR firm or become the manager of a national firm's local office are solid, experienced professional public relations practitioners who have excellent planning, writing, media relations and client relations skills.

However, like every rule, there are exceptions to this one. For example, there is the insurance executive who inherited his mother's PR firm and succeeded in this new field. There are the corporate planning executive and the officer of a software manufacturer who teamed with their PR-professional wives to create flourishing technology firms.

There are no rules or statistics covering the minimum number of years' experience required to become a firm principal. However, personal experience and observation tells me that you should have at least three to five years experience as an underling before seeking or attaining the top rung or going out on your own. Five to eight years of agency or corporate experience makes the leap into the bull ring that much more comfortable.

Some agency principals arrive directly from corporate backgrounds, either to scratch a nascent entrepreneurial itch or because they were down-sized out of an executive position. However, individuals with an agency background will have an easier time accepting and adapting to the pressures of agency leadership than a corporate emigrant. There are subtle differences between the personality and motivation of individuals who naturally belong in a corporate atmosphere and those whose light burns brightest at the helm of an agency. I have long felt that if you were to stack 100 PR practitioners in a room, 45 of them would naturally lean toward corporate employment, 45 would function well in the agency business and the other ten could be successful switch hitters.

Why so? Doesn't the agency principal have the same professional responsibilities as his corporate counterpart? Don't both individuals strive to develop and implement public relations programs that meet client/employer objectives and produce excellent results? Of course. However, two distinct and unique needs set every agency principal apart from a corporate PR executive.

Agency principals (and staff members as well) are driven by a dominating and sometimes demonic need to be "billable"; to be productive; to bill the majority of their time to clients at a profitable hourly rate. (At this writing, it has been seven years since I filled out my last agency time sheet and became a consultant to PR firms. And yet, I still feel guilty when confronted during working hours by moments when there is absolutely nothing I have to do.) Concerned agency principals/professionals also strive to reduce client costs by whisking through assignments in the shortest possible time consistent with good quality.

In addition, agency principals face the prospect that, sooner or later, every client is likely to either cut budgets or disappear for reasons totally out of the principal's control. To simply maintain cash flow equilibrium, much less grow the firm, you must constantly seek additional business either by increasing income from current clients through new assignments or by winning new clients, generally under competitive conditions.

These demands focus extreme pressure on the agency principal, pressure not likely to be matched in a corporate venue. As a result, corporate PR executives entering the agency world often encounter severe culture shock. (In a reverse twist, many experienced agency principals would likely feel a sense of emotional jet lag if they tried to pare down to a more moderate corporate pace.)

No matter what their backgrounds, successful agency principals have one thing in common. They are very smart people who thrive under the heat and glare of PR firm leadership.

PERSONAL DEDICATION AND RESILIENCY

Successful agency principals must be dedicated to 60/80-hour-plus work weeks, few or no vacations and slim pay checks when times are tough (and that's the good news). You must be able to accommodate (without resorting to violence) overbearing, incompetent, inconsiderate clients (who hopefully and thankfully will be few in number). You must accept gracefully that not every employee will be as competent as you expect. Many are likely to do things differently than you. This is not necessarily a bad thing. Few will be as dedicated to your agency's future as you.

To cope comfortably with such adversity, you must be supremely confident of your own personal strengths and professional capabilities. Conversely, you must also be so comfortable in your ego that you have no problem recognizing, admitting and accepting gaps in your experience or abilities, and in taking steps to fill such gaps.

You must possess in massive quantities the capacity to bounce back; to pick yourself up off the floor of defeat or despair one more time. And then do it again. You must recognize that not every client will approve your best recommendation or applaud your best effort for reasons that you may never understand. You must accept that a prospect's failure to return your phone call does not mean that he or she hates you. You must not be insulted when the prospect does not know who you are after you've sent him several letters and have left phone messages for a month. And you must recognize that losing a new business competition does not mean that your firm is less competent than the winner.

MANAGEMENT INTEREST AND SKILLS

She leads a high-flying specialty PR firm that is one of the most innovative and best known in its market. And yet it has high staff turnover and low profits. She sits at her desk during a quick lunch break in an all-day meeting and silently screams, "I hate to manage!"

The very creative juices and counseling strengths that make many PR firm principals so successful as public relations advisors and generate heady client enthusiasm often conspire to weaken the firm's management structure and bottom line health. The sense of excitement and risk-taking vigor that drives an entrepreneur toward seemingly unreachable goals often drives employees wacky. They long for consistency and rhythm in the work place while the entrepreneur quickly tires of routine and longs for new directions to explore and new heights to scale.

While the firm is young and emerging from its cocoon, the principal's lack of business management interest and ability may not be noticeable or harmful. But give the firm a little success, a little growth, more staff members and it begins to cry for management structure and direction.

And then you, the entrepreneur, must either become a manager, find a senior back-up who can fill the management void . . . or expect possible employee turmoil and a bottom line that does not reflect your best interests.

Example: A southern firm led by an affable entrepreneur with extensive community contacts and professional respect struggled with before-tax profits barely into one digit. Two years after the entrepreneur sensed the problem and recruited a senior practitioner as his chief operating officer, before-tax profits had risen to 15 percent and a substantial new employee bonus program was in place.

MARKETING AND SALES INTEREST AND SKILLS

An old agency axiom contends that there is no problem that a little new business will not fix.

Somewhere in this world, there may be a public relations agency to whose bosom clients rush with desperate need and mindless trust.

An agency for whom a competitive new business "pitch"– a stand-up oral conflict in which your opponents may be three to six other equally hungry firms–is unknown; where all the new business that can be handled rolls in as easily and uninvited as if forwarded by the Good Witch of the North. There may be such a firm, but I have never seen nor heard of one.

For the most part, badly needed new business–new clients to flush away despair and restore confidence–will not follow some magical automatic directional finder to your front door. It must be sought out, chased after and often fought for.

New clients must be pursued with purpose and consistency and stamina and bravery. Cold calls–perhaps the most dreaded part of any shy principal's day–must be made to unresponsive prospects. Your quest for additional business must be organized to take best advantage of your firm's strengths as well as to open up opportunities in new fields. And you must seek new business while you are the busiest fighting fires and otherwise meeting current clients' needs. Because despite your best efforts, your best client may not be with you tomorrow . . . and must be replaced.

TAKE THE GOOD WITH THE BAD

In your life as an agency principal, there will be good days and bad days. Hopefully, more of the former than the latter. On good days, you will rejoice in the independence of not reporting to anyone (except your banker) or perhaps only a distant executive. There is tremendous satisfaction in knowing that if anything good happens, it probably happened because of something you did, either directly or by training or motivating someone else.

The satisfaction of leading a group of loyal, skilled, enthusiastic people is hard to match. (Consider the emotion generated when 30-some people applaud as you exit an elevator on crutches after a month-long surgical recuperation. This is lumps-in-the-throat stuff.)

You will wallow happily in new business triumphs. A long-sought prospect who phones to say, "We've decided to go with your firm," will light a fire in your heart and spark exultation of the highest order. Time for a staff party! (Always, always celebrate wins. There will be enough times when you cannot celebrate.)

The good days also bring peer recognition; days when your firm is ranked higher than previously on a list of local or national PR agencies, or you win an industry award. (I still remember that Saturday morning–a lot of years ago–when the Public Relations Society of America called my Milwaukee home from New York to say that our firm had won a coveted Silver Anvil for a public affairs program on behalf of Harley-Davidson Manufacturing Company.) Clients may even find reason or occasion to compliment your firm's work. Cherish these occasions!

If you apply the right client service, new business and agency management principles, the opportunity for financial gain is excellent–despite the sweat you will manufacture each month as you worry through the cyclical nature of the agency business. It is not unheard of for even small firm principals to take home more than $200,000 annually in salary alone, not to mention benefits and perks.

Ahh, but the bad hair days! Come they will. Sometimes with such frequency and intensity that you will plead mournfully "I need something good to happen!" or "I need a win!"

Small firm principals who migrate from large national firms sometimes spend many of their days yearning for the large clients with big budgets and extensive ambitions whom they formerly served. Now, their client list may consist largely of local companies whose small budgets are matched only by their lack of PR sophistication. Many times, unsophisticated clients are also unprofitable because of the excessive demands that they make on your time combined with your willingness to let them do this if only to help keep the lights burning.

One of the reasons you will need to keep the lights burning is so that you can see to work while you're putting in all the extra hours that will be needed. Managing the business and wooing possible new business will take many of your daylight hours. That leaves the other side of the clock for client work that must be completed, including meeting unrealistic deadlines.

One of the reasons you may have trouble meeting client deadlines is because of a shortage of really competent people, particularly at the salary levels that you will be able to afford when your firm is young. (And because most university PR graduates know how to solve the Three Mile Island crisis, but they do not know how to write a new product release or make up a media list.)

Your monthly "numbers" will be the cause of some of your worst days. If you are the manager of a unit of someone else's firm, you may only have to answer tough questions when earnings fall short of objectives.

But when your name is on the door, it's a different story. When client budgets are cut (count on it, they will be), expected new clients do not come in when you expect them (prospects' priorities will never be the same as yours), and the monthly nut exceeds the cash in your bank account, calamity will ring its bell. Then your short-range solution may be an American Express card or your home in hock for a bank loan. Why go through all this when maybe you could get–or keep–a cushy corporate job? Because, in the first place, if you are a true agency person, you will be bored out of your skull in the corporate political arena. In the second place, being an agency principal gives you far more opportunities to win than lose.

Winning is what the game is all about; whether it is a media coup on behalf of a client, beating another firm in a heated competition for a new piece of business, generating the blackest possible bottom line or watching a talented but raw young account executive develop into a polished and competent professional.

If you are good at your job, the days that you win will sustain you in the days that you don't. But if you are not good, if you do not have strong professional, entrepreneurial and management interests and capabilities, then you might better save time and stick your head in the oven in the beginning because the end result will be the same.

THE NEW BUSINESS GAME

Aside from assuring a high level of client service, the days of a successful PR firm principal–your days–will be filled with marketing your firm for growth and managing your firm for profit.

First, marketing your firm for growth; that weird, frustrating and eminently satisfying process also known as "new business development." Unlike other contact sports, it is not how you play this game, but whether you win or lose. The following pages offer some hints as to how the game is played and how you can win more often than you lose.

PART II.
MARKETING YOUR FIRM
FOR GROWTH

PROFILE 3

RICHARD BLEWITT, PRESIDENT, ROWAN & BLEWITT, WASHINGTON, DC

Backed by 15 years of newspaper and chemical industry PR experience and armed with a retainer-plus-hours contract from his former employer, Rich Blewitt and partner TV newscaster Ford Rowan opened an issues and crisis management firm in 1984. (Blewitt was one of the few corporate PR executives to beat *60 Minutes'* Mike Wallace to the draw when Wallace drew a bead on Velsicol Corporation, Blewitt's former employer.)

In addition to developing and helping implement strategies on sensitive issues for such clients as General Motors, Bic, and Hoechst Celanese, the firm offers opinion research, government relations and crisis and media training (some through a subsidiary, Executive Television Workshop). In ten years, the firm's income jumped from $300,000 to $5 million. Blewitt's business plan calls for the firm to hit $10 million in another three years.

The firm is very low-profile. "Our clients like it that way," says Blewitt. "They like the fact that we do not normally list our clients or publicize the sensitive work that we do." The firm participates in few competitive presentations.

Blewitt's number one frustration is the volatile nature of crisis counseling. To balance this volatility, the firm cross-sells all its services, including those of R&B Services, a video and print production affiliate, and uses a "value added" pricing strategy that calls for a premium fee or bonus payment for success.

Chapter 3

Anatomy of an Agency Search:
How the Game Is Played

THE BEGINNING

Every week, somewhere in the United States, invitations to a unique tribal mating dance are issued to public relations firms by corporations and institutions. Corporations call this dance an "agency search." PR firms call it a "new business pitch."

It is a dance in which the partners may never have met but during which they exchange intimate details of their business lives. It can result in a relationship that is long-range and mutually fulfilling or short-range and mutually disastrous. It also can determine whether a corporation achieves its public relations objectives and whether a public relations firm grows and prospers.

This is the story of a hypothetical agency search from the viewpoints of The Company and The Agency.

THE SITUATION

ABC Inc. is a large, well-established Company with nationally advertised brand names and a reputation for solid, growth-oriented management. The Company recently completed a dramatic and comprehensive recapitalization and restructuring to avoid a hostile takeover. The successful takeover defense resulted in a substantial debt load that will require ABC Inc. to cut costs, lay off a number of employees, and sell several subsidiaries.

The Company needs to communicate the strength and goals of the "new" ABC Inc. to employees, shareholders, customers, vendors and the financial and banking communities. Jan Jones, ABC director of public relations, recommends that a public relations firm with national capabilities be retained. Because the Company has never used a national public relations firm and she is not familiar with the PR agency community, Jones also recommends that the Company retain a management consultant to coordinate the search for a competent and compatible firm. Management agrees.

THE SEARCH

The Company

March 1-March 4 . . . Jan Jones and the consultant meet with key ABC executives to discuss the Company's public relations objectives and the agency search process. The consultant suggests that the Company talk to no more than six agencies to not only provide a variety of choices for the ABC Review Committee but to make it easier for the Committee to identify and remember each firm's distinctive character under the pressure of competitive agency presentations.

March 15 . . . The consultant submits a draft of the Request for Proposal (RFP) that will be given to counseling firms as the basis for their presentations. The RFP contains: an outline of the Company's history; a description of the takeover battle and the resulting recapitalization and restructuring; a review of the objectives and target audiences for the planned public relations program; a description of criteria to be used in evaluating prospective agencies; a preliminary timetable for the search process; and a list of recommended agencies. The consultant also supplies an outline of the recommended agencies' credentials and capabilities and explains the rationale for each firm's selection. (One ABC executive questions the absence of a national "name" agency from the list. He accepts the consultant's reasoning that the agency's strength and reputation lie primarily in consumer product marketing not in the communication areas that will be required in this assignment.)

March 21 . . . The approved RFP, inviting competitive presentations, is sent to six agencies. One of the national firms on the list declines to participate because of a client conflict in another office. Another firm with strong credentials is invited to compete. The final six agencies include the local offices of three international organizations, two independent firms and, at the request of the Company, the public relations department of the Company's advertising agency.

The Agency

March 22 . . . Agency General Manager Bob Smith receives the RFP and calls the consultant to express his appreciation for the opportunity and to arrange a briefing meeting (offered in the RFP) with Jan Jones and other ABC executives. He also reviews the RFP with two of the Agency's senior executives and they develop questions to be asked during the briefing meeting.

One of the firm's executives begins to gather accounts of the takeover battle from local newspapers and business publications and a national data base resource.

March 30 . . . Bob Smith and his two senior executives meet with Jan Jones and ABC marketing and financial officers. Bob also asks for a brief, get-acquainted meeting with the ABC President and CEO, who will be part of the Review Committee.

The Company

March 28-April 1 . . . Five of the agencies on the list meet with Company executives. The public relations department of the Company's advertising agency does not request a briefing. Rather, the head of the advertising agency calls ABC's vice president of marketing, indicates his interest in being considered for the public relations assignment and says that his agency probably knows the Company well enough that they don't need to take anyone's time in a meeting.

Based on the briefing meetings, the ABC executives form opinions about the five agencies and begin to consciously rank the firms in terms of their ability to meet ABC needs. They are very impressed with the personalities and professionalism of two of the firms' executives and respond positively to the astute questions asked. An ABC executive wonders out loud whether the final agency choice will match the ranking that is already shaping up.

The Agency

April 2-April 27 . . . All six agencies will present in their offices on April 26 and 27. The Company Review Committee will visit each of the firms' offices to get a feel for agency ambiance as well as to observe staff activity levels. Dates and times for the six presentations are drawn at random. The Agency will present at 10:00 A.M., April 27. They will be allowed one hour for the presentation with an additional half hour for Review Committee questions. Bob Smith is not particularly pleased with his time slot because agency industry lore says it's better to present to a prospect either first or last to ensure memorability. However, he would rather present in the morning than after lunch when the prospect's attention span may be affected by full stomachs, tired posteriors or information over-load.

The Agency begins to prepare its presentation. A staff member thoroughly researches the Company, its industry, markets, audiences, market share and the details of the takeover battle and resulting recapitalization and restructuring. A telephone survey is conducted of editors, industry leaders, financial analysts and bankers to determine their awareness of the takeover defeat and their understanding and attitude toward the Company's status following the takeover attempt.

A small group of Agency executives and senior staff members brainstorms public relations approaches to the Company's needs and Bob Smith begins to gather case histories on other successful Agency campaigns that will show the ability to solve similar problems. He meets briefly with the ABC president and gets a slightly different impression of the CEO's goals than was gained from the briefing. He calls Jan Jones for a clarification and asks some additional questions that arose in the brainstorming session.

Bob begins to draft the presentation script, leading with a situation analysis, the results of the Agency's preliminary research and a brief description of the Agency's capabilities. Most of the presentation will be devoted to recommendations for a public relations program to meet the Company's goals. He times the script as closely as possible to 55 minutes.

The draft script is reviewed and revised, and a rough run-through of the presentation is held for timing. Bob decides that since the Company is rather conservative and has never worked with a major public relations firm, a "dog and pony show" with elaborate computer-generated audio and visuals will not be appropriate. Instead, he opts for an attractive flip chart outlining points that the presentation team will make. A short videotape of television news placements for other clients will be shown during the Agency capabilities section. Agency presenters will use the flip chart as a guide rather than reading from a script.

April 26 . . . Tomorrow's the pitch! The script and flip chart are completed. The presentation team, including Bob Smith, the account supervisor and the account executive who will be assigned to the business, rehearse several times to polish their delivery and make sure they will be able to stay within the allotted hour. Several senior staff members sit in on the final rehearsal to comment and pose questions that the Review Committee may ask. It is decided that Bob Smith will answer all questions directly but that other members of the team should feel free to add appropriate comments.

A typo on one page of the flip chart is discovered and corrected. There is a discussion of appropriate dress for the presentation: what should the female account supervisor wear; does it matter whether Bob Smith and the account executive wear the same color suit? The office manager is asked to have coffee, tea and rolls available. The staff is alerted to clean up messy offices. A secretary begins to print and assemble copies of the presentation script for the Review Committee. Special binders have been obtained with the Agency's and the Company's names and logotypes embossed in gold. Everyone agrees that they are as ready as they are going to get.

Mid-afternoon! The consultant calls and asks if the Agency's presentation can be moved up to 9:00 A.M. the next morning so that the Company CEO can have additional time for an important lunch meeting. Bob Smith agrees and informs the Agency team.

A few minutes later, a new piece of information comes in from a source who was not available earlier. It needs to be included in the presentation. One page of the flip chart must be changed. Since the new information goes in the up-front, situation-analysis section of the script, all the following pages will have to be renumbered and reprinted. Bless word processors and laser printers! (The secretary cancels an after-work date.) Inserting the new information will not run the presentation overtime, if one of the case histories is trimmed.

Another rehearsal is held in the evening to make sure that the new material is handled properly and that the timing is still within one hour. Everyone goes home late, but feeling that the additional information makes the presentation stronger.

The Company

April 26 . . . The Review Committee meets at 8:00 A.M. to be briefed on the criteria that the management consultant has suggested they apply in evaluating each agency. Information on each agency's address, executive staff, background and experience is distributed. (A list of the Review Committee's names and titles was sent previously to each agency.) The consultant, who has an extensive agency management background, has developed a list of questions that Committee members may want to ask the agencies.

The Review Committee arrives at the first agency, one of the international firms, 15 minutes late and is taken on a tour of the premises before the presentation. Some office doors are closed, prompting one Committee member to wonder whether the offices are vacant or occupied by busy people who do not want to be distracted.

There is some shuffling in the conference room as Committee members are asked to take seats that place them on one side of the table facing five agency staff members. The presentation is opened by the firm's president, who has come in from agency headquarters. He expresses his pleasure at being considered by ABC Inc., introduces the other staff members, and shows a 15-minute videotape of the firm's national capabilities. (One member of the Committee is impressed by the fact that the national president has come in for the presentation; another wonders whether the president's presence indicates a lack of confidence in the local management.)

The president is followed by the local general manager who describes the firm's emphasis on research and creativity and covers a couple of quick case histories of local office accomplishments. An account supervisor, assisted by two account executives, launches into a series of public relations recommendations that include positioning the Company CEO as a highly visible corporate spokesperson. (The CEO, who hates to speak publicly, winces inwardly.) The agency finishes ten minutes over the allotted time. Copies of the presentation book are passed out and the firm's president asks for questions.

The Committee is silent, waiting for the Company president to lead off. His question takes the general manager off guard and requires about ten minutes to answer. There is more silence. A Committee member glances at the list of questions provided by the consultant and picks one. Another Committee member follows suit and two other executives ask questions of their own.

One executive turns to the budget page in the back of the presentation book. He underlines the total recommended dollar figure and shows it to another executive, widening his eyes in alarm. The general manager catches the gesture and quickly explains that the budget represents only a "Chinese Menu" that will be finalized after priorities are set and financial parameters established.

Committee members thank the agency for its time and interest. The consultant asks that the Committee be permitted to use the conference room for 15 minutes while they complete the 15-category, 150-point, Qualification Audit that he has prepared.

The agency's general manager and visiting president wait in the lobby to bid the Committee good bye and thank them for coming. As the elevator doors close, a passing account executive asks, "How'd it go?" "Pretty good, I think," the general manager says. "Yeah," says the president, "No one threw up."

The Committee visits two more firms after lunch, tours premises that are similar to the first agency (except that there are no closed office doors) and listens intently to the presenters. Some Committee members always ask the same questions.

As the Committee leaves the last presentation of the day, there is a consensus that one of the firms has taken an early lead. An executive jokes, "Why don't we just pick them and forget about sitting through tomorrow?"

The Agency

April 27 . . . Bob Smith and his team arrive at 8:00 A.M. to make sure that everything is in order. The account executive discovers that, somehow, the pages in the presentation book are out of order. The three hurry to rearrange all the books.

The first member of the Committee arrives at 8:45 just as the receptionist is setting out the small sign that reads, "Welcome ABC Inc." By 9:05 A.M., all the Committee are present. After a tour of the office (Bob is thankful that most of the staff members are at their desks despite the earlier schedule), Bob welcomes the guests, introduces the other two members of his team, notes that everything that will be said is covered in writing and invites questions during the presentation.

The account supervisor discusses the Agency's analysis of the Company's situation and describes the results of the survey. The last minute piece of information from an important financial analyst stirs a discussion among the Committee members. Bob uses this discussion to lead into a description of other work the Agency has done that was aimed at the financial community. This stimulates several more questions. Bob decides to eliminate the rest of the capabilities section and the videotaped TV news clips because they are running long. He introduces the account executive.

Even though this is only the second time the account executive has participated in a new business pitch (only he knows how nervous he really is), he handles his presentation smoothly; segueing from Agency recommendations that respond to the Committee's obvious interest in the financial community to other aspects of the recommended program. Also recognizing that the presentation may go overtime, he manages to shave some minutes without losing his place in the flip chart outline.

Because of the discussion and questions, Bob's conclusion, including "We're ready to go to work tomorrow," goes slightly over the allotted 60 minutes. The Company president leaves, but the rest of the Committee ask questions for another 17 minutes and spends 15 minutes completing the Qualification Audit.

Bob agrees with the supervisor and account executive that, despite all the problems, the presentation went well. He congratulates the account executive on his professional delivery and for being able to shorten his part of the presentation so smoothly.

The Company

April 27 . . . The last two presentations are uneventful but uneven. One of the firms offers a number of creative ideas that are not related to strategies linked to the Company's objectives. The public relations director of the Company's advertising agency, who has drawn the last time slot, recommends activities that appear to be based primarily on the Company's marketing program. The Company's marketing vice president comments later that he had been surprised when the firm passed up the opportunity to meet with Company executives.

The Agency

April 28 . . . Bob Smith messengers a letter to all the members of the Review Committee that briefly reviews the Agency's presentation and emphasizes its ability to help reach and influence the financial community. He works on another new business pitch that will take place within the next week.

Staff members ask how the presentation went and when the prospect will make a decision. Bob answers, "Pretty well, I think. They asked a lot of questions," and "I don't know. Soon, I hope." (He remembers, "Good news comes by the telephone; bad news comes by the mail.")

The Company

May 10 . . . The Review Committee meets to select an agency. (The CEO has been out of town all the previous week.) In the meantime, three of the six Committee members, including the CEO, have read all the presentation books supplied by the competing firms.

The consultant has tabulated all the Qualification Audits completed by the Committee and arrived at an average score for each firm. The Committee discusses the six presentations while the president does not comment. Discussion centers primarily on three questions: how interested the agency appeared to be in the Company's business; how smart they were about the Company and its needs and how well their recommendations relate to those needs;

and whether the agency representatives' personalities appear to match the Company's culture. For the most part, the Committee agrees that all the agencies appear to be professional and personable. However, the Committee is particularly impressed with the expertise and enthusiasm displayed by one agency's general manager and account executive and the creative and strategic strengths of their recommendations.

Concern about the high cost of one agency's recommendations is mentioned. An executive notes that he upgraded his opinion of one firm after reading the firm's presentation book. One firm is criticized for offering a plethora of creative ideas not supported by strategic direction.

The competing firms are ranked one through six by the Committee and this consensus is compared to the Qualification Audit average scores. They match. The president finally expresses an opinion. He concurs with the Committee consensus and the Qualification Audit scores and indicates his preference. The Committee makes a decision.

May 11 . . . Jan Jones makes a telephone call to the winning agency, congratulates the general manager and asks him not to say anything until the other firms have been notified the next day by mail. She sends nicely worded consolation letters to the other firms.

The Agency

May 11 . . . Bob Smith gets a telephone call from Jan Jones, expresses his pleasure, thanks his new client for the business and arranges a start-up meeting. He swears the supervisor and account executive to secrecy until the next day and asks the office manager to lay on an office celebration for late the following afternoon.

May 12 . . . Bob Smith gets a call in the morning from one of the other competing agency principals who congratulates him on the win. The principal has not received his letter but he has heard "on the street" that the Agency has won. Late in the afternoon, Agency staff members are called to a meeting where Bob announces that they have won a substantial new client. He congratulates the supervisor and the account executive and thanks everyone for their help. Champagne is poured. (The Agency did not win the second pitch that Bob was working on but he figures that one out of two is better than none.)

The Other Agencies

May 12 . . . The consolation letters arrive. In several cases, word of the defeat is passed to staff members. Two managers call Jan Jones to thank her for considering them and to ask what the Committee had based its decision on. "It helps us in the future if we know what the deciding factors were in cases where we did not get the business," one manager says. The Company director of public relations is vague; she says, "The Agency seemed like they would be better able to meet our needs." (Her favorite did not win.)

The five losing agencies swallow their disappointment. One manager tells his staff members that they did a great job and he's proud of them. He says he would not do anything different if he had it all to do over again.

All six agencies continue their eternal quest for new business.

ANOTHER ENDING

The Agency

May 11 . . . Bob Smith knows the ABC Review Committee met yesterday to select an agency. He tries not to think about that while helping to solve a client problem and preparing for another new business pitch scheduled for the following Monday morning. He waits for the "good news" telephone call.

May 12 . . . Before the mail arrives, an account executive tells Bob that she has heard from friends the night before that another agency has won the ABC business. A letter arrives from Jan Jones. Bob calls to congratulate the head of the winning firm.

Bob then calls Jan Jones to thank her for the opportunity to be considered and ask what the Committee had based its decision on. The ABC director of public relations is warm and friendly. She says it was a very close race and a tough decision but the Committee felt that the winning firm had done a slightly better job of addressing the Company's needs. She invites Bob to stay in touch for possible future opportunities. (The Agency was her favorite.)

Bob asks the supervisor and account executive into his office and informs them of the loss. He congratulates them on their effort and says he wouldn't have done anything differently. In an E-mail message, he informs the staff of the decision, comments on the great job done by the supervisor and account executive, thanks the secretary for her overtime assistance and says he thinks the Agency has a good chance in the competition coming up the next Monday.

The five losing agencies swallow their disappointment. All six firms continue their eternal quest for new business.

FOOTNOTE

The two firms who made the best impressions during the first briefing meetings finished one and two in the competition. Well balanced culture compatibility, expertise, enthusiasm, creativity and strategic thinking, plus the Committee's "gut feeling," won the day.

It could have . . . in fact . . . it probably did happen that way.

PROFILE 4

HOWARD BRAGMAN, PRESIDENT, BRAGMAN NYMAN CAFARELLI, BEVERLY HILLS, CA

Frequently named a "hot creative shop" by industry publications, the firm serves a unique blend of entertainment and corporate clients (Whoopi Goldberg, Coca Cola Company).

While a national agency executive, Bragman saw opportunities for a firm that was results driven, could handle clients paying under $10,000 a month and could work on a fixed fee and keep expenses down. Using this approach, the firm has moved from $100,000 in 1989 income to $1.5 million.

"If clients don't meet at least one of four criteria, I walk away," says Bragman. "It's extraordinarily lucrative, you can always find a way to do it; If it's something you know very well, it means you can get results quickly; If it's something you are passionate about or really believe in; or If it's something you can build on.

"I've worked very hard to not only do good work, but to not do bad work. As an entrepreneurial company, we don't have to meet a particular number every quarter. We have the luxury of saying, 'No, it's not right for us.'

"Because of our location and the fact that the partners had both corporate and entertainment experience, we felt that there would be good synergy in a combined approach. It's easier to learn the entertainment language if you have the basic corporate skills. That's why we could help a company like Coca Cola with their 'Oscar' program for Fresca."

Chapter 4

Developing a Marketing Plan

If you rely for sustenance and growth only on current clients, referrals and over-the-transom inquiries, sooner or later, you will find that revenue has plateaued or begun to slide. Set a goal; spend at least 40-50 percent of your time actively seeking additional business.

Realistically, if your firm is small, client needs may restrict the amount of time that you can devote to new business development. However, it is vital that you make time available–as much as possible, as regularly as possible–to plumb for growth opportunities.

Because of the cyclical nature of the agency business, the most important–as well as the most difficult–time to pursue new business is when you are the busiest with current clients. Unfortunately, you may lift your head at the end of an intense client campaign or project only to realize that no more work will be coming from that client for some time or discover that other business has dried up while you were heavily involved with several clients.

As difficult as it may appear at the time, devoting disciplined, consistent and substantial time to business development will pay huge dividends over both the short and long run. In fact, it could make the difference between your firm's success or failure.

To apply your limited time most productively, combine rifle shot and scatter gun approaches to new business solicitation. There is no need to go after or accept every piece of business that falls your way. Be selective. Decide the kind of business you want and take your best shot at it.

To provide direction and priorities, invest the time to develop a definitive, realistic marketing plan that outlines an on-going promotional and solicitation program. Include these ingredients in your firm's marketing plan:

ASSESS AGENCY STRENGTHS AND WEAKNESSES

Evaluate your firm objectively. Consider utilizing an outside consultant to add objectivity.

What are your strengths? Technology, media relations, crisis response management, investor relations, special events, experienced senior management back-up, business-to-business experience, consumer product marketing background, distinctive culture, low staff turnover?

Look at every element and aspect of your organization that could be of value to a client or that could help convince a prospect that you can do a better job than competitive firms in serving his or her needs. Write down the strengths of your firm. Also, while being brutally candid write down a list of weaknesses and holes in your organization. Describe your limitations in detail. Again, you might want to ask a consultant to help you analyze your firm's fragility.

No senior back-up? Limited experience beyond one or two areas? High staff turnover? Shabby or cramped quarters? Inexperienced staff? Little or no experience serving major large budget clients? Don't ignore the warts. List every aspect of your agency that might possibly persuade a prospect that he would be better off awarding his business to another firm. Note the effect these weaknesses could have on your ability to acquire new clients. Do the weaknesses cancel any of your firm's strengths? Can the weaknesses be cured? How? How long will it take and how much will it cost? Is it worth doing?

Develop a realistic plan, budget and timetable to eliminate or ameliorate the weaknesses. And do it!

Business development efforts needn't be put off until all your firm's weaknesses are eliminated. Simply take the warts into consideration while preparing the remainder of your plan and in implementing your promotional campaign. (Walk around the stone wall until you're strong enough to knock it down.)

EVALUATE SERVICE POTENTIAL

What kind of services could you provide with your current staff that you are not providing now; special events, publications, promotion, employee communications? Make sure that you are fully aware of your staff's past experience. For example, would a staff member's experience preparing annual reports provide an opportunity to offer limited investor relations services to current or new clients? What kind of additional services could you provide by making some staff changes? Think about such possibilities when you hear about or interview good people.

EXAMINE MARKET POTENTIAL

Analyze your market or industry intensely and comprehensively to determine the hot service areas. It's one thing to offer additional services such as consumer marketing or investor relations. It's another to be sure that the need is there. Otherwise, you'll waste a lot of time and money.

Consider using a blind telephone survey of PR executives to garner information on the kinds of services that are valued by companies in your market, what services companies are currently buying from competing firms and what they wish was available. In addition, use the survey to learn how the corporate PR community regards leading PR firms in your area, including your own.

How big is your market? In terms of miles and dollars? How far can you afford to travel to serve what size client? When expanding a Chicago firm's reach some years ago, I decided that every company with at least $50 million in sales and within one hour's flying time or three hours driving time was a potential client and belonged on my mailing list.

Today, the list would probably cut off at $100 million and two hours flying time. (But not more driving time. It is too tiring and time wasteful.)

All of this depends, of course, on the size of the client's budget and how often he or she expects to see you in their office . . . and how badly you want the business.

We served a major Los Angeles consumer product client successfully from our Chicago office with no logistical problems and satisfactory profitability. West Coast technology firms commonly and easily serve Midwest and East Coast clients. With the advent of fax machines, modems and interactive computer software, distance is probably more a problem in a client's imagination than in reality. The likelihood of a client needing to see you frequently on very short notice (minutes, rather than hours) should determine how far away you can afford to be.

The extent of your market potential lies primarily with your own personal choice, your agency specialties and your prospects' willingness to be served long distance. Obviously, if you're located in Minneapolis, it will be more convenient and efficient to reach prospects in that city than in New Orleans. However, New Orleans is not out of reach. Be aware, though, that when you reach out beyond arm's grasp, you will then be competing with all the local firms *on their turf*.

Here are some other questions to ask when analyzing your market. Check *O'Dywer's Directory of PR Firms* to find the companies in your market area who use counseling firms. Do the companies who make your mouth water currently use other PR firms? Who? How? Is your firm more or less competent?

CONSIDER THE PROFIT POTENTIAL

Many firms set minimum annual income or minimum project income that they will accept. ($60,000 minimum annual income per client is a good bogie. The larger your firm, the larger your minimum should be.) Income potential should be a prime factor when determining the viability of a prospect. However, an even more important factor when prioritizing prospects is the prospect's profit potential. Some generalities apply:

- Small business-to-business clients–in fact, most business-to-business clients–can be just as profitable percentage-wise if not dollar-wise as large consumer product clients. Small clients are often easier to handle because of less complex demands.
- However, small, unsophisticated companies, particularly start-up companies backed by venture capital, can demand almost as much of your time as a large company. They also may be reluctant to pay higher hourly rates and may nitpick invoices.
- A client that requires a heavy investment of your most senior peoples' time will lean toward low or no profit unless you can

convince the client to accept an hourly rate that returns full profit. (Because they would probably not be competitive if computed realistically, many seniors' rates are not profitable. Junior rates, on the other hand, tend to be very profitable.)

Establish profit potential guidelines in your marketing plan. Consider the above generalities and your need for a consistent profit level when adding or subtracting companies from your mailing list or solicitation schedule.

ANALYZE COMPETITION

One of the most important aspects of your new business effort will be your understanding of the reality and reputation of other PR firms in your market. Use that knowledge in competitive quests for new clients. This in no way suggests that you attack or criticize other firms. That tactic will sink your ship faster than almost anything else you can do wrong.

On the other hand, understanding the strengths and weaknesses of firms you may be competing against can help steer your presentation in a direction that will shine the best light on your firm.

Get to know your competition personally. Meet as many of your potential competitors as you can, given the number of firms and geographical spread of your market.

What are the principals like? Are they low-key or high pressure? Are they casual or formal? How good are they? What are their professional backgrounds, strengths and reputations? What kind of new business presentation do they normally give; informal, across-the-table or heavy on glitz and audio visual?

Participate in local chapters of the PRSA Counselors Academy or independent groups of agency principals. For example, in each of three cities where I assumed responsibility for faltering or non-existent PR firms, one of my first moves was to organize an invitational group of local agency principals so that I could get to know my competition. *Chow & Gab*, a monthly luncheon group of about 40 PR firm principals that I founded in 1983, still functions in Chicago at this writing. Similar groups exist elsewhere.

There are some obvious things to consider when analyzing your competition: (1) size; (2) national, international or network ties;

(3) leadership; (4) senior strength; (5) service specialties or strengths; (6) size and type of clients.

There also are other more subtle pieces of information that will be helpful. What is the firm's reputation, not only among corporate public relations executives, but among senior corporate officers as well? (In one Midwest city, a national firm's general manager had good contacts with corporate CEOs, but was not generally well liked by corporate PR executives. Competing firms used that fact to make subtle points with prospects.)

Is the firm's leadership active in community service, in the social or cultural communities? (If a firm's leader or senior management is active in community cultural organizations–the opera, ballet, symphony orchestra–will that give his or her firm an advantage with a prospect who is also active in the same organization or who would like to gain a prestigious community board seat?)

Is the competing firm growing, shrinking, or static? Is it going after smaller clients than it had been? What is the word on the street about the firm as a place to work? Does it have a number of long-term employees or heavy staff turnover? Why the latter? (You can gain valuable information about other firms during interviews with their employees or former employees. Is the firm highly structured or more collegial? Is client contact restricted to senior people or broadly encouraged? Why does the practitioner want to leave?)

Are there cultural differences between your firm and others that are worth emphasizing? In *Butch Cassidy and the Sundance Kid*, Robert Redford and Paul Newman are pursued by an unknown but seemingly indefatigable posse. As they top a rise with the dust of the posse close behind, one of the pair asks plaintively, "Who are those guys?"

My upstart Chicago firm, seeking to position itself in a market jammed with well-known local and national outfits, used that line as our business development theme, symbolizing our "unknown but coming fast" culture. In four years, by emphasizing this kind of employee spirit combined with hustle, strategy-based creativity and a targeted new business campaign, we became the tenth largest firm in the city.

DEVELOP A UNIQUE STRATEGIC POSITION

Now that you have assessed your firm's strengths and weaknesses, evaluated the potential for additional services, examined the size and peculiarities of your market, looked at income and profit potential and analyzed competition, it is time for the most important part of your marketing plan.

Develop and communicate a unique strategic position that describes your firm succinctly and persuasively and takes into account what you know about your competition. Decide how you wish to be seen by clients, prospects and the PR community. Set down the words that you will face up to and live by and which–if you do the job right–will drive your firm into prominence and profit.

What is your firm all about? What makes it different? What will prospects see that they will like particularly well about your firm? What kind of working philosophy do you live by? Here is one firm's strategic position (that I'm most familiar with because I wrote it and lived it):

> " 'Good Enough' is Not Good Enough. In today's business marathon, no corporation, institution, association or other organization can afford to settle for 'adequate' when it comes to public relations service. *Exceptional has to be the least acceptable standard . . . without exception.* The public relations service you receive determines how you are viewed and judged by investors, customers, employees, suppliers, regulatory authorities . . . the worlds in which you work.
>
> "Here's how we define exceptional: Powerful resources; Strategic planning strength; Fresh, creative ideas; Work ethic style; Honest value; Full range of services; Worldwide services; and Outstanding people."

The cover of the firm's brochure carried one word: "Exceptional."

That was a general strategic position. There are others–more market or specialty specific. With some elaboration, "The best health care firm in the area with a long list of well known, long tenure clients," could be one.

In Philadelphia, a market molded in the who-you-know, establishment "Main Line" image, my firm fought to be different and to be noticed.

Our strategic position was largely internal . . . to create a charged atmosphere and motivate employees to excel. Rock the boat. Up the establishment. Be unique. Sometimes raucous.

Emphasize competence, creativity and experience. (No practitioner had less than ten years experience. That's not practical today.) New employees conquered the toughest writing test in the city and their pride showed. We took our work very seriously but laughed a lot at ourselves.

In a loud and bustling ambiance with few private offices, we functioned with noisy enthusiasm. We hustled. Shouted messages–some crude, some funny, most team oriented–across the partition walls. Assigned women to technical accounts. Unthinkable then. Esprit soared. Staff turnover was unknown. So was client turnover because we produced results. And in five years, from a stumbling four-man crew, we became the second largest in the city.

How will your firm be seen? Incorporate your vision in your market plan, and then tell the world about your firm.

PROFILE 5

HERBERT CORBIN, MANAGING PARTNER, KCSA PUBLIC RELATIONS, NEW YORK, NY

Four years with a national PR firm led Corbin to a strong belief that typical PR firms were structured wrong. "We're in a service business; all we have to sell is our time. If you tell a client that senior people are going to be accountable for his work, you better have those people around. The person can't be here one day and gone the next."

When Corbin founded the firm in 1969, he followed this philosophy, developing a horizontal management structure in which senior partners–now ten of them–are responsible for the management and implementation of each account, much like a law firm operates. The partners relate directly to each client and manage the day-to-day work of supervisors and other practitioners.

Corbin also believes that every client requires at least 40 hours per month to produce results. Fees are set to cover at least this minimum number of hours. In addition, the firm uses only two average hourly billing rates. The first 40 hours each month may be billed at the lower rate while all hours over 40 may be billed at the higher rate. "With this system, we can assign senior people to each client at affordable costs and sustain good relationships," Corbin says.

The system works. KCSA has grown from $100,000 income to about $4 million and is rated one of the best managed firms in the country.

Chapter 5

Communicating to Prospects

Because your firm has existed for several years does not mean that it is well known within the business community in general or among prospective clients specifically. If your firm is relatively young, you can assume that very few have heard of it. Most senior executives and many public relations directors tend to have only a vague knowledge of the counseling firm community. In fact, some companies know so little about the extent and variety of available firms that they turn to the Yellow Pages when seeking a counseling firm. (Buy at least a boldface listing for your firm.)

The fortunate firms, those who have at least some degree of recognition and credibility, are the large national firms, long-tenure mid-size firms and smaller firms who invest the time and money to create effective self-marketing programs. To maintain or increase your firm's visibility . . . and improve your potential for growth . . . it, therefore, behooves you to use every available avenue and apply every affordable tool to communicate your firm's capabilities, culture and achievements to a targeted group of prospects.

Marketing your firm should be easy. Right? All you need to do is apply the same kind of communication techniques on behalf of your firm that you recommend to your clients. No sweat, right? Wrong!

Unfortunately, the "Shoemaker's Children" syndrome frequently gets in the way of a firm's self-marketing efforts. There's always something that keeps you from communicating with prospects as often or as well as you should. Client demands; lack of cash; lack of objectivity (face it, it's tough to be objective and say nice things about yourself); or maybe you just don't know how to do it. Forget these excuses. Here is all you need to know to design and carry out an effective self-marketing program.

BE VISIBLE

If you don't do anything else, make time to join groups where you can meet and talk to prospects. Your current clients may even be impressed when you attend a meeting of the local business association (especially where your client's CEO is president or is speaking).

If you are going after primarily local clients, Kiwanis, the Lions Club, and Chamber of Commerce are good sources. Join national trade associations covering industries that you're interested in and attend their conferences and trade shows. Join the Public Relations Society of America (as well as its Counselors Academy), the International Association of Business Communicators, the local publicity club and maybe the American Marketing Association.

Get involved in these groups; run for office, chair committees, lead programs, if that is your thing. (It never was mine. I knew it was a good idea, but I'm not a committee person and I don't function well in most groups.)

A better idea, one that I was always more comfortable with, is "pro bono" (meaning no charge) work for worthy charitable, civic and cultural organizations. In addition to being a good public service thing to do, the people you meet in these organizations are the same ones you would probably meet at the Kiwanis or PRSA.

WRITE AND SPEAK

Use your writing, speaking and public relations skills to find and take advantage of opportunities to appear before target prospect groups or write articles for publications reaching prospect audiences.

For instance, if you'd like to have a bank as a client, offer to speak before a bankers' group on a subject you're familiar with and that the bankers would find interesting and useful. (How to increase the return on their PR budget.) In the same light, offer to write an article for a bankers' trade publication (same subject). National, regional and local business, marketing and sales publications offer good article placement opportunities.

Most important, keep your article or speech 99 percent non-commercial. Concentrate on information or ideas that demonstrate how well you know the topic and the particular industry for whom you're writing or speaking. Prospects will get the idea that they ought to talk to you without you beating them over the head about how great your firm is.

This is all so basic that I hesitate to even mention it. However, the fact is, not all that many PR firm principals take advantage of speaking opportunities unless they're approached by a group looking for a speaker or a client pressures them to help fulfill his or her program chairperson obligations. The truth is that many PR firm principals are not the greatest speakers in the world and need their knees tied together when addressing a large group. Practice!

When you write an article or speak to a group, be sure to reprint the article or speech and merchandise it to your clients and prospects. Use "Third Party Credibility" in your behalf as well as your clients.

In the same vein, publicize agency events such as new client wins, creative awards, significant anniversaries or milestones, personnel hires, an acquisition or merger with other PR firms or industry survey results. Send news releases to local business journals, newspaper business editors and/or the advertising/PR columnist, if there is one, and to well-read national public relations publications such as *Jack O'Dwyer's Newsletter*. Get to know your local newspaper or business journal's advertising/PR columnist. Your growth story, awards, comments on business practices or unique approach to client service may warrant an interview and column coverage.

TREAT EMPLOYEES AND APPLICANTS WELL

You may not think of human relations as a communications channel. However, your relations with current and prospective employees play an important role in the way your firm is viewed by prospects and others in the business community.

To a great extent, because of the multiple contacts that your employees have, the business community will tend to see your firm the same way that they do. If employees categorize your firm as a "sweat shop," whether this is fact or fiction, you may be sure that many others in the PR community will be exposed to this pejorative comment. If your firm has excessive staff turnover, others will wonder why and may invent "reasons" that have no relation to the truth.

In the same light, if your firm has a sudden run of client departures or budget cuts that require staff layoffs, the rumor mill will have you in bankruptcy almost before the ink dries on the first termination notice.

For these reasons–beyond the positive impact it will have on staff morale, employee productivity and, in the end, your profitability–treat employees as if you were the originator of the Golden Rule. Remember that in the public relations community in particular, and in the business world in general, people–especially your competitors–are always ready to hear, believe and pass on negative information about your firm. Don't give them that opportunity.

Prospective employees are another thing. Treat every person that you interview or who asks for an interview as if they were about to become a prospect with a $500,000 budget. Even if you have no openings, take time to interview candidates. (This also will give you opportunities to learn more about your competitors and local corporations.) Treat every candidate with the same respect and courtesy that you would a prospective client. There are two reasons for this.

First, one-year-out-of-college, can't-spell-Mississippi job candidates have a way of suddenly gaining substantial experience and significant corporate credentials, not to mention large budgets. People have long memories about the way they were treated by a prospective employer. It makes good business sense to ensure that job candidates only have good memories of your firm.

Second, the way you treat candidates will affect your ability to attract the best possible staff members. Job candidates sense the way your firm is run by the way they are treated in an interview. It is hard enough to find good people. Why turn them off by treating them badly during the interview or refusing to even take their call requesting an interview?

I would practically have laid my neck on a railroad track for Andy Anderson, then-president of Ketchum Public Relations in Pittsburgh, PA, who said gently, "We'd like to persuade you to come to work for us." He wanted to *"persuade"* me to come to work for him? Who do I have to kill?

In later years, I often had job candidates come back for a second try or become a prospect after they were treated fairly and politely when either they did not qualify or there was no opening. In one instance, a young woman said, "You told me I needed another year's experience. I have it. I would like to talk to you again." She became one of our most competent account supervisors.

USE BUSINESS CONTACTS

There are several other groups of people who can help communicate a positive message about your firm to prospective clients. Some of these also can be good leads to companies who are actually looking for a PR firm. It is important that they all have a good opinion of your firm.

- *Trade publication space reps*–Although you may not have much direct contact with individuals who sell print advertising space, they are a great source of information about companies who may be disenchanted with their current PR firm or actively looking for a new one. It may pay to take a space rep to lunch once in a while.

- *Editors*–Companies often ask newspaper or trade publication editors for opinions about a specific PR firm or recommendations of firms that the editor respects.

- *Vendors*–Printing salesmen, VNR producers, photographers, graphic artists and other vendors to the public relations industry also tend to have a good feel for companies that are looking for a PR firm and are often asked for their impression of specific firms.

- *Clients*–Many PR firm principals will tell you that they get most of their new business from client referrals. It's probably wishful thinking. However, clients who like what you do for them, also talk to other prospective clients. Hopefully, they will not hesitate to recommend your services. There's nothing wrong with telling clients that you will appreciate business referrals.

- *Other agencies*–Agencies often learn of companies that are either too small for them to handle, that conflict with other clients or which, for some reason, they cannot accept or are not interested in. It is common, in such situations, for the original firm to either refer the prospect to other specific firms or to tell other firms about the prospect. Stay friends with your competitors.

MINE SOCIAL AND CIVIC ACTIVITY

Personal friends and contacts made in pro bono civic and cultural work can provide good leads to new business. These people should have a positive impression of your firm.

Urge your employees to keep their ears open during social situations and their negative comments to themselves. A social hour before a business meeting, a cocktail party, your table mates at an industry dinner or fund raiser, can all be good sources of new business leads. Keep your ears open and your mouth closed when riding in an elevator. More than one new business tip has come from listening to elevator conversation.

COMMUNICATE REGULARLY

Listen to the advice that you give clients. Communicate consistently to prospects. Ideally, they should hear from you at least every six to eight weeks. If you publish a newsletter, do it at least quarterly. Anything less and you might as well spend the money on a lottery ticket. (On second thought, you'll also probably have better luck at the lottery if you buy a ticket regularly.)

One of the goals of your communication program should be to establish memorability for your firm with prospects. Sell them on the benefits of public relations and your ability to meet their PR needs. These are both good objectives. However, the real reason for communicating consistently is to hit prospects at the exact time that they are ready or thinking about hiring a new PR firm. In that light, marketing your firm should have more than a little bit of scatter gun approach to it.

You should have a small list of prime targets whom you contact regularly and personally. However, most of your prospects will be little more than names on a mailing list. Qualified names, yes, but still little more than names about whom you know little, especially their need or interest in retaining or changing PR firms.

So load a shotgun with your most powerful ammunition and fire it regularly in the direction of the people that you have defined as prospects. If your message is strong and you shoot often enough and your luck is good, you will hit some targets. (Lesson for the day: This is why a hunter does not usually shoot a rifle at a flock of geese. And why he likes to take more than one shot at a flock.)

Make it easy for prospects to communicate with you. Be sure that your telephone and fax numbers are on every printed piece in a type size large enough to be read easily. Enclose a postage-paid return card with every communication. Ideally, your return card should give prospects some choices: Send more information; call me immediately about a specific subject; call me on a specific later date; send me a list of clients; keep me on your mailing list.

There's a reason for the latter. Of course, you are not going to remove prospects from your list just because they do not signal that they want to remain. However, when a prospect indicates that he wants to be kept on your mailing list, you can bet that, in most cases, you have hit a nerve and that somewhere, perhaps hidden in the back of his mind, the prospect has or will have a need for a PR firm.

Your immediate written response should be, "I'll be delighted to keep you on my mailing list. Even though you don't have a need right now, I'd like to come by and get acquainted and tell you a little bit about our firm. I'll call you for an appointment." (Despite the fact that the prospect has returned a card to you, he may not remember your firm's name. Therefore, it is better to reinforce the name to him in writing rather than try to reach him immediately by phone.)

Once in his or her office, you have a great opportunity to probe the prospect's needs and to turn an unknown name into a client.

FOCUS YOUR MARKETING PROGRAM

Much of your marketing program may necessarily take a shotgun approach, aimed at reaching a broad multi-faceted audience. Therefore, your marketing materials should describe your firm's ability to serve varied markets and multiple client needs. On the other hand, you will want to be able to customize a package of promotional materials to appeal to a specific prospect. Many firms satisfy this need by developing an attractive "kangaroo" folder that can be customized by inserting a general agency brochure plus material such as letters, reprints, photographs and case histories tied to a prospect's specific interests.

Add to the need to customize material to match prospects' interests the need to fit within their culture as well. Examples: The public relations manager of a large Midwest manufacturer of marine engines chortled over the three-piece-suit-clad national agency representatives from Chicago who ventured to the manufacturer's Lake Michigan test facility. And who then managed to look uncomfortable, scared, and silly–and somewhat seasick–with tie, coattails and hair whipping in the wind as they clutched the top of a boat's windshield on a high speed run across the lake. A telephone would have explained the manufacturer's lack of a dress code. They didn't get the business.

In a similar incident, national agency representatives descended on an outdoor writers' national conference clad in suits and lugging stacks of an elaborate 24-page agency brochure for distribution to the group of relatively small outdoor product manufacturers attending the meeting. They were promptly labeled "Arrogant!" by the very people they were trying to impress.

DUAL PROSPECT LISTS

There are two kinds of prospects: (1) those that are referred to you or come in "over the transom" because of your firm's reputation; and (2) those that you target and solicit. The first type is usually the easiest to convert to client status; the second is the most difficult, and usually the most expensive, to win, yet perhaps the most satisfying. Your new business prospect list–a vital tool in your quest for new clients–should contain as many names as you can qualify within your target markets. Building and maintaining a new business prospect list is a boring, time-consuming pain in the neck, make no mistakes about that. Your list will be only as valuable as it is accurate. Strangely enough, the anticipated labor and time required to build and maintain an accurate list is probably one of the biggest reasons why any PR firm does not have an effective marketing program. The principal never gets around to seeing that an up-to-date list is assembled and maintained.

You have two choices in building a list; you can buy one from a list broker or assemble your own. Buying is faster, but you have no guarantee as to accuracy of the names on the list. Doing it yourself or assigning it to someone else (maybe an intern) is slower, but probably more accurate and can be customized to reach exactly the audience that you are interested in.

I prefer the do-it-yourself approach, although I'm sure the modern, computerized approach is easier. In Chicago, I built and maintained two different lists based on the same corporations located in six Midwest states: one contained CEOs; the other listed marketing, sales, and public relations executives. Manufacturer, association, and Chamber of Commerce directories and the "Red Book" of corporate advertising clients will give you information on which to base your lists. You may need to make telephone calls to update information.

Side note: Every time you use your list, particularly if you mail material third class, ask the Post Office to not only forward the mail but also provide forwarding addresses so that you can update your list. About 5 percent of my list of agency principals changes every time I use it.

Your list should actually have two parts: the largest portion will be those with whom you maintain regular indirect contact, largely through direct mail. This is the "B" list. The "A" list may contain no more than ten or 20 names. These are your high priority targets. The people on this list have either previously indicated a possible need for a PR firm or fit your definition of a prime prospect; a company or institution whose name you passionately want to see on your client list. This list should comprise only as many people as you can comfortably contact regularly and frequently, preferably at least monthly.

Contact these individuals in person, by phone or personal letter–initially to qualify them as potential clients. If, after several months, you sense that there is no possibility of converting a company to a client in the near future, move it to your "B" list and switch another "B" name to your "A" list.

Try to visit or otherwise personally reach out to each "A" individual at least once a month. Learn as much as possible about the company; invest in secondary or data base research on the company and its industry. In addition to such accepted approaches as brief "get acquainted" meetings, lunches, breakfast and after-work socializing, here are some other techniques that will help win a prospect's heart, and most important, build memorability for your firm:

- If a prospect company hires a new out-of-town PR executive, welcome him or her to town; invite them to accompany you to professional group meetings; invite the executive and spouse to dinner with you and your spouse or significant other;

- Congratulate individuals on promotions;

- Comment on industry events and/or trends; suggest ways to take advantage of opportunities or help solve industry problems;

- Forward articles about the prospect's industry that they may not have seen; comment on the articles;

- Respond to favorable publicity on the company or offer suggestions to help ameliorate negative publicity; and

- Be interested in the prospect's company. Show it! Consistently!

Example: After 18 months of fervent pursuit with only lukewarm response, Harley-Davidson Manufacturing Company, the last U.S. motorcycle manufacturer, became a major client on 48-hours notice for a national public affairs campaign that eventually won the agency and client a PRSA Silver Anvil. At this writing, about 15 years after the abrupt start-up, Harley-Davidson is still a client of that agency.

THE DIRECT WAY

One of the best and, yet, most difficult ways to reach and interest prospective clients is through direct mail. "Best" because it offers an effective and relatively economical method of communicating to a large number of people using a shotgun approach. "Most difficult" because your mail piece must compete for time and attention with the mass of other material that lands on your prospect's desk every day. Unless yours is extremely well done and aimed precisely at the prospect's interests, it will be ignored or consigned to the infamous "round file."

This volume is not intended to explore the intricacies of direct mail. Your local library or book store undoubtedly has at least one good book discussing all the most potent tricks and tactics of direct mail. (A direct mail expert-friend recommends *The Do It Yourself Direct Mail Handbook* by Ray Raphel and Ken Erdman, published by Raphel Publishing, 12 S. Virginia Avenue, Atlantic City, NJ 08401.)

Remember that in order to be noticed and read, your direct mail must appeal to a reader's interests and needs. The piece must give the recipient some reason to read it other than the fact that it shows up on his or her desk. Here are some direct mail tools that may prove useful:

- A letter accompanying a brochure or other mailing piece is reputed to increase the return over a no-letter mailing.

- Case histories that take a problem/solution approach to work you have done for clients can be very effective, particularly if they can be applied to a prospect's specific needs.

- Small brochures that fit in a Number 10 envelope are more practical and effective than a single large brochure because they require less reading time.

- Reprints of articles you've written, speeches you've given or other favorable publicity about your firm should be reprinted (with the publication's permission if necessary) and distributed broadly to both current clients and prospects.

- Newsletters can be very effective if done properly. The most effective newsletters are published regularly and emphasize information that interests and benefits prospects. Their sole purpose should not be to pat the agency on the back. Unfortunately, many agency newsletters seem to be published primarily to aggrandize the agency's principal.

COLD-CALL MARKETING

"Cold calling" makes the sweat pop out on many agency principal foreheads. At its best, prospecting for new business opens up the potential for rejection. (No one likes to be rejected whether by a lover or a business prospect.) Cold calling doubles, maybe triples, that potential. Few principals like it. Most are not very good at it. But many–this writer included–force themselves to do it.

Industry surveys would have you believe that most PR firms get their new business primarily through referrals; i.e., it falls over the transom or is referred by kindly clients. However, according to New York consultant Lee Levitt, principals of a number of the largest PR firms do not rely on referrals, but do cold-telephoning regularly and personally.

PR firm principals like to say that they get most of their business from referrals, according to Levitt, because it sounds good and implies that a firm that gets clients primarily through referrals must not have to seek them out. These principals may be concerned that people will think that a firm that uses cold-call marketing techniques is hard-up for business or that it is (perish the thought!) "pushy," according to the consultant.

Levitt claims that cold calling generally brings in better clients more economically than any other sales technique because it allows you to go after the clients you want to serve and can serve profitably now. Conversations start on your timetable at your convenience. You talk to prospects most likely to appreciate what you have to offer. And you establish the terms of the discussion at the outset.

Levitt supports my belief that many PR firm principals are not comfortable with the idea of "imposing" on an executive's time to sell him something he may not need or want. (Twenty-five years of agency experience and lots of new business success never quite cured me of this phobia.) But, says Levitt, many corporate executives have a sales mentality and react well to cold sales calls.

Levitt lists these keys to successful cold-call marketing:

- A strategy that targets an industry or field;
- A reasonably good knowledge of that field/industry;
- A carefully researched contact list;
- A "gimmick" to grab the prospect's attention;
- Relevant material to send interested prospects;
- Knowledge of telephone-solicitation techniques;
- A good telephone manner, feeling for people and patience; and
- Commitment.

Chances are, you will have to do some cold calling–you may even like it–and face that potential for rejection. Remember what we said earlier in this book: The successful agency principal ". . . must possess in massive quantities the capacity to bounce back; to pick yourself up off the floor of defeat or despair one more time. And then do it again." (A favorite line of Depression-era radio comic Herb Penner fit the cold-call trauma perfectly. Playing a sad sack door-to-door salesman, Penner would intone, "You wouldn't want to buy a duck, would you, Mister?")

I found that sending a letter to a prospect several days before my call took some of the onus off the task. At least it gave me a wedge into the conversation assuming that my letter had been persuasive enough.

EXPLORE TELEMARKETING

There is a way to avoid cold calling yourself and still accomplish the same end. Telemarketing has been used successfully by a number of firms primarily to qualify prospects and arrange appointments for firm principals.

Two relatively small firms–Davis, Hays & Company, Maywood, NJ, and Smith & Shows Public Relations, Menlo Park, CA–both used staff telemarketers to conduct highly active and successful new business development campaigns.

There were a number of similarities between the two firms' telemarketing campaigns:

1. Female employee with telemarketing, not PR, experience;
2. Use of telemarketing for about three years;
3. A targeted approach to prospect qualification; and
4. Primary objective–appointments for firm principals with qualified prospects.

Most significantly, both firms reported that telemarketing was a key ingredient in their growth. Here's how each firm used the technique:

Davis, Hays & Company, Maywood, NJ

The firm's telemarketer worked on a salary-only basis for 15 hours a week. She not only made prospect telephone calls, but wrote initial and follow-up letters to prospects and participated in regular staff meetings to become familiar with firm operation, client activity and success stories.

Working with principals Alison Davis and Betsy Hays, the tele-marketer developed customized prospect lists of Fortune 500 companies based on the firm's experience and success stories.

"We tried to leverage our experience in a specific area to gain other clients in the same area," says Davis.

A customized letter was sent with work samples to about 25 prospects at a time. The telemarketer called each prospect to determine PR or internal communication needs and interest in meeting with the firm principals. The telemarketer set the appointment but did not attend the first prospect meeting.

An average of five appointments were obtained for every 200 letters, Davis estimates. Prospects who did not have an immediate need or interest, but who might have future potential, were placed on a computerized "warm" list that prompted follow-up calls. There were generally several hundred names on the list.

"Follow-up was crucial," says Davis. "Most people were not interested immediately and it could take as long as 18-24 months to arrange an appointment with a warm prospect." The telemarketer arranged 25-30 appointments a year for the principals.

The telemarketer had a good background in the firm's current activities as well as written thumbnail descriptions of the firm's successes. When a prospect showed no interest in one area, the telemarketer switched her query to another area in which the firm was experienced.

Two of the firm's three major clients at the time resulted from the telemarketing campaign as well as about three-quarters of its other clients, according to Davis.

"The turning point came when Betsy and I recognized that we hated to follow-up with prospects by phone," says Davis. "With telemarketing, our new business effort became more consistent and we had better control of it."

Smith & Shows Public Relations, Menlo Park, CA

Smith & Shows' telemarketer had similar responsibilities: to make initial contacts, qualify prospects and arrange appointments for the principal. (Firm president, Winnie Shows, also makes 25-30 calls per week to "warm" prospects and says she "likes doing it," proving that there is an exception to every rule.) The telemarketer, who had telemarketing experience with a high tech company, worked full time on a salary plus commission.

The firm, which specializes in a specific area of high tech PR, has about 2,500 companies on a software data base. (A big problem with many firms: a poor or no prospect list.)

At this writing, the firm ". . . has had some contact with about 1,500 prospects," says Shows. "We made as many as ten calls to many of them and at least four times a year with most of them." Contacts made at trade shows went on the prospect list for follow-up. A "tickler" system prompted the timing of follow-up calls. The firm also sent a quarterly newsletter and occasional marketing letters to prospects.

While an investment of time and money is required to get a telemarketing program working successfully, Shows is enthusiastic about the results. "We could trace at least 40 percent of our annual revenue at that time to the telemarketing program." "However," she advises, "Don't attempt it without a long-term commitment to training and computer systems."

After achieving management goals, both firms cancelled or cut back their telemarketing programs. Other firms continue using basically the same technique.

Secrets to Success

To be successful, a telemarketer should:

1. Be well organized, a part of your team and fit into your culture;
2. Be excited about your firm and feel a personal stake in its success;
3. Be interested in public relations, even if he or she has no experience in the field;
4. Have good writing skills, especially the ability to write good prospect letters; and
5. Have essentially the same skills and personality as a good media placement specialist, including the ability to talk to hostile people and explore various alternate new business possibilities.

If you plan to hire a telemarketer, you might want to conduct much of your interview over the phone–rather than in person–to see how the individual comes across. (Winnie Shows listed a voice mail box telephone number when advertising for a telemarketer.)

THE GROUP APPROACH

PR firms often recommend that their clients sponsor a seminar as an effective, noncommercial means of reaching potential and current customers. You can use the same technique with good results on your own behalf.

Pick discussion subjects of broad interest and on which you or one of your senior staff members has in-depth knowledge and experience. A seminar could cover such topics as "New Regulations Affecting Initial Public Offerings"; "How to Introduce and Position a Commodity Product"; or "How to Satisfy Your CEOs' Demand for Measurable Return on PR Investment."

Invite a small group of editors and PR and/or marketing executives (clients as well as prospects) to attend a breakfast or late afternoon discussion of the selected topic. Serve coffee and rolls or light refreshments.

Either give a short presentation yourself–not more than 30 minutes–or invite an outside expert to discuss the seminar's topic. For instance, if your budget is tight, you could invite a newspaper business editor, a client's vice president of marketing or a local investment banker to meet with seminar participants. If the budget will allow it, a nationally known expert will attract a larger attendance.

The seminar should be noncommercial with no obvious plugs for your firm. Give each participant a package of material on your firm and let it go at that. Later, you will want to follow up with a phone call to each participant.

CAPABILITIES PRESENTATION

Sooner or later, a prospect will call at 3:00 P.M. and ask to meet with you at 9:00 A.M. the next day. Or the prospect that you've been chasing for months will finally agree to see you or visit your firm. This could be your big opportunity. Don't get caught short in such situations.

To respond to prospect requests or for get-acquainted meetings that you schedule, you should have a brief–15 to 20 minutes–in-the-can capabilities presentation ready to deliver to prospects on short notice. The presentation should be casual but well scripted. It should describe your firm's strengths, unique strategic position and results that you have obtained for clients. While much of the presentation will be standard, you should be able to easily and quickly customize segments for specific prospects by changing elements such as case history examples.

Depending on your facilities and/or those of the prospect, you may want to incorporate slides, video tape and/or computerized material in your presentation.

Communicating regularly to prospects is half the job of winning new business. The other half consists of an array of sometimes mystical truths and techniques, all aimed at influencing prospects to pick your firm above all others. Read on.

PROFILE 6

ROGER FISCHER, PRESIDENT, FISCHER & PARTNERS, MARINA DEL REY, CA

Fischer & Partners is a glowing example of an agency taking advantage of the times. The firm was founded in 1983 as Pollare/Fischer Communications (Partner Frank Pollare left the agency business in 1992), changed to Smith/Fischer & Partners in 1992 and reformed as Fischer & Partners in 1994.

"In the 1980s, we built a mid-size independent firm that was clearly a generalist," says Fischer. "The 1980s rewarded mid-size generalist firms. There was enough business for everyone, particularly for an agency that was highly visible locally and was regarded as a 'hot' agency.

"However, the 1990s demand increased specialization, particularly from mid-size firms. The only way to be all things to all people is to be a megafirm. To succeed against these new demands, we decided to spin off our consumer product group and specialize in two areas: Healthcare and Electronic Media. We now offer broader services to narrower segments of the marketplace."

Annual agency income has grown from $150,000 to about $1.6 million while serving such major clients as American Express, Polaroid and Toshiba.

"Our early success was probably attributable more to the boom years than a brilliant strategic plan. However, we did learn that you ignore the 'business of the business' at your peril. Our focus on specific industries is a direct result of client demands for increased specialization."

Chapter 6

New Business Rules

During 25 years hustling business for three PR agencies, I learned two very important Rules:

1. Never Work in the Dark;
2. Never Put Your Prospect to Sleep.

If you follow these two Rules, you will consistently win more than your share of new business–because many other firms do not adhere to the same rules. In fact, some agencies act like the rules read "Always Work in the Dark" and "Always Put Your Prospect to Sleep."

NEVER WORK IN THE DARK

In the dim, dark days before computers, this writer was a public relations vice president for a national advertising and public relations firm (an agency, incidentally, that fully appreciated the worth and profit potential of public relations and the power of a combined advertising and PR campaign). On one memorable occasion, I was scheduled to make a brief pitch on behalf of PR as part of a major presentation to a large advertising prospect who had indicated no interest in public relations.

I don't recall the prospect's name. However, I vividly recall fretting nervously outside the conference room door as my appointed time approached. The agency president was leading the presentation and I wanted to make a good impression. Finally, the door opened and a hand waved me in. Inside, the room was totally black with only a dim glow lighting the podium.

I laid my script on the podium, tried to see faces in the dark and began my pitch. And was suddenly stricken with dismay! "What the heck am I doing here?" I thought. "I don't know anything about these people; they don't know anything about me or what I am talking about and could care less. I'm wasting their time and mine with this bland plea on behalf of public relations. (Herb Penner would have been proud of me.) "This is dumb! I am not going to do this anymore. I will never work in the dark again." And I never did. From then on, I refused to present to a totally dark room. More important, I always made sure that I learned enough about the prospect to make my comments pertinent to his business. When I began running my own PR agency show, "Never Work in the Dark" became a new business development credo.

MORAL: Always take the time to learn the prospect's business, markets and industry–so that you can look smarter and more interested in the prospect than your competition, and so that you can do a really top-notch job of extolling the rewards of a public relations investment. This is especially necessary when you are talking to someone who thinks primarily in terms of advertising, either paid or "free."

NEVER PUT YOUR PROSPECT TO SLEEP

As the head of a growing Philadelphia public relations operation, I traveled to the Midwest to pitch the owner of an automotive products company. By this time, I had about ten years experience in the agency business and was pretty impressed with myself, particularly my ability to convert prospects to clients.

I was ushered into the office of the company president, a gray-haired gentlemen wearing a number of summers. (In those days, in the callowness of youth, people always looked older to me than they probably were.) That we were in the president's *office* was the first surprise. I had assumed that we would meet in a conference room. But here we were in his office where he sat behind a huge desk festooned with layers of paper.

I looked around the office for the easel on which I could stand the carefully prepared flip charts that I carried in a "pizza case." Second assumption gone wrong. No easel. (In those days, I also didn't know enough to make sure that the accessories I was going to need in a presentation were available at the prospect's location.)

So, improvising, I balanced the flip charts across the arms of a large straight chair in front of the president's desk and launched into my pitch. (Of course, that meant I had to hold the flip charts with one hand while I turned pages with the other. Awkward!) The president continued to casually thumb through the rat's nest on his desk, with hardly an eye skewed in my direction. Not too encouraging.

Even less encouraging was the moment I realized that the reason he had stopped rearranging papers on his desk was not because he had become fascinated with my golden offering, but because he had fallen asleep. Head nodding on his chest. There was nothing to do but fold my tent and creep silently out of the room. (A lot of years later, and now a consultant to PR firms, the president of an East Coast agency fell asleep during our meeting. But at least this one wasn't bored; she suffered from narcolepsy.)

MORAL: Always aim your proposal and presentation directly at the prospect's interests and needs rather than spending excessive time discussing your firm's capabilities and conquests. Talk in terms of benefits to the prospect rather than extolling the virtues of your firm or the services you are trying to sell. Do not put your prospect to sleep by dwelling on things that he or she is not interested in. (Try not to present after lunch or in the middle of the afternoon. It's nap time.)

DESIGNING A NEW BUSINESS CAMPAIGN

I also learned that to be successful in soliciting new business, you should:

1. Commit to a Consistent and Substantial Investment of Time in the Quest for New Business

Time is generally in short supply in most agency principals' lives. However, time is a vital element in every successful new business campaign. You should devote a good chunk of time regularly–40 to 50 percent of your time–to planning the campaign, compiling and maintaining the prospect list, writing or supervising letters, literature and other mailers, making cold calls, making warm calls, and preparing proposals and presentations.

If you only remember one thing about new business development, remember that the most important time to press for new
business is when you are the busiest with current client work.
Bringing in a new client usually takes much longer than you expect
or would like. To avoid the cash flow gap that can occur when work
dries up from one or more clients, you need to press continually for
additional business, either from a new client or from new areas
within current clients.

2. Conduct a Focused, Organized and Budgeted Self-Marketing Campaign

One of the biggest mistakes made by PR firms is failure to
conduct an effective and ongoing self-marketing and new business
campaign. The "Shoemakers' Children" syndrome at work again.

When a firm comes up short in the cash flow department, the
principal may decide that the answer is to attract some new clients.
(By this time, however it may already be too late to solve the cash
flow problem comfortably.)

Naturally, to attract new clients, you need an agency brochure,
literature, case histories or article reprints. However, just producing
the brochure can take months, not to mention the time necessary to
develop the mailing list that the piece will be sent to. Then the firm
gets busy with client work again. Cash is flowing.

Everybody forgets about the self-marketing campaign. No one
calls anyone on the firm's prospect list; no one pays any attention to
the postage-paid cards that possible prospects have sent in (assuming that you remembered to include such a card with each mailing);
no one spends any time planning the next promotional mailing.

Another mistake is the failure to adopt and adhere to a self-marketing budget. Between 1 and 2 percent of projected annual income
is a realistic figure for new business expenses. However, if your
firm is young and in a growth mode, you may want to budget 3 or 4
percent of your income. Plan your self-marketing budget–from both
time and out-of-pocket standpoints–the same way you would a
client's budget.

Don't leave your self-marketing program to chance; something
you do when you have nothing better to do. If you do not conduct a

consistent self-marketing campaign, you may very well end up with nothing else to do. And then it will be much too late.

3. Act Smarter Than Your Competitors

The truth is that, on the surface, public relations firms seem pretty much alike to many corporate PR executives. Agency offices tend to look alike; the same cluttered desks, the same pile of press kits in the corner of the conference room, the same stains on the coffee room counter, the same people huddled over glowing computer monitors.

PR firms even tend to say the same things to prospective clients. They promise day-to-day service by the principal; they say they are big enough to provide a wide range of services but small enough to care about each client; they say that they are creative; and that "we are ready to go to work for you tomorrow."

What they need to say is, "Here is what we have learned about you. Here are the problems you told us about and some others that we see on your horizon. Here is how we recommend that you solve your problems and take advantage of your opportunities."

Want to look smarter than your competition? Want prospects to pay more attention to you than your competitors? Couch everything that you say and do in terms of your prospects' needs. It's that simple.

SELF-MARKETING CAMPAIGN ELEMENTS

Your firm's self-marketing and new business campaign should contain equal measures of:

Research

Remember "Never Work in the Dark." That advice–in effect, get to know your prospects–applies whether you are attempting to break into a lucrative new industry or are pitching an individual company.

Planning

Organize your thinking. Plan your overall campaign as well as each individual presentation and proposal. Leave nothing to chance;

especially remembering to take extra extension cords when you're pitching in the prospect's conference room.

Strategic Creativity

Strategy-based creative ideas win the day every time. Unsupported "Big Ideas" get little applause. PR firms that are strong in strategy win; firms that are only function-strong lose . . . sooner or later.

Positioning

How do prospects and clients see your firm? How do you want to be seen? As a generalist; as a niche market player? How are you different, really different, from other firms? Define your firm's strategic position in 25 words.

Intensity

New business solicitation is not something to be taken lightly or approached haphazardly. It requires emotion, purpose and seriousness. Impress the prospect with your integrity, character and intelligence. Demonstrate that you are interested in the long haul, not the greatest profit in the shortest possible time.

Commitment

Keep at it. Fight back against disappointment. Learn to live with rejection. Dedicate yourself to success. Do not accept less than your best effort. Encourage others to emulate your commitment.

Focus

Decide what you want and go after it. Brush aside easy pickings that could pose profit problems. Waste little time trying to teach public relations to the unwashed. Seek clients that offer fun, profitability and professional satisfaction.

PROFILE 7

TOM GABLE, CHAIRMAN/CEO, THE GABLE GROUP, SAN DIEGO, CA

After ten years as a business editor, founder Tom Gable changed careers in 1976 so that he could stay in San Diego instead of being transferred to the East Coast. Gable believed that a market existed for a PR firm based on his experience on the receiving end. He felt that most public relations services were being provided by semi-retired advertising executives. It turns out he was right.

From first year's revenue of $45,000, the firm has grown to 30 employees, income of $2.3 million and a reputation as one of the best managed and most progressive medium-size PR firms in the country. (The Gable Group's "Client Service Manual" is so good that other firms buy it.)

To be successful, Gable says principals must: "Hire the best available talent, even if they cost more than you want to pay; make a change quickly, if you feel that an employee is not right for the firm; and provide consistent quality and performance."

If he was starting his firm today, Gable says he would take more management classes at the post-graduate level and learn to be a better manager sooner. He also would be more targeted in networking and new business efforts.

Gable advises principals to: "Establish a mission for your firm; train, manage and motivate your team to achieve the mission; and focus on measurable results."

Chapter 7

New Business Secrets

The most important secret about winning new business is hardly a secret at all. Unless you prefer to remain small, so that you can be heavily involved in client service, prospecting for and winning new business must be one of your most important, continuing tasks.

However, even small firms must be able to gain new business. It's no secret that the agency business tends to be highly cyclical and unpredictable. Clients depart or reduce budgets with little warning and for reasons that cannot be controlled or even explained at times.

On the other hand, there are some secrets to gaining new business that are not so well known or practiced. For example: how to win business against the big PR firms if yours is a small one; how to cold call prospects successfully; how to use computer data bases as a competitive advantage; the kind of questions you should ask prospects; and the kind of mistakes that prospects make during an agency search (so that you can watch for them and turn them to your advantage).

TEN WAYS TO BUILD BUSINESS

The late nationally-known "consultant to consultants" Howard Shenson, in his *101 Proven Strategies for Building a Successful Practice*, recommended:

1. Add sales letter impact with a handwritten P.S.
2. Don't hesitate to charge for problem diagnosis and needs analysis.

3. Spend half a day, at least twice a year, walking around the reference room of a major university library. You will learn about interesting marketing opportunities and new services that you could offer.
4. Devote half a day each month and call people who could be prospects for your services or good sources for referrals whom you have not talked to in the last six months.
5. If you have developed a proposal for new business that fails, identify others who would benefit from such services or ideas and recycle your proposal.
6. Multiple page sales letters usually out-pull single page letters. Interested prospects will read a great deal and the extra copy increases response.
7. Increase your credibility by recommending that your services not be used for certain needs which the client or prospect may have, but which can be met internally.
8. When meeting with prospects, be sure to answer the five questions that they need to have answered, but frequently fail to ask: How will I profit from your advice/services? Why will I profit from working with you? How can you demonstrate that I will profit? To what extent will I profit from your advice/services? When will these profits/benefits be realized?
9. Don't beg for the business. No one wants to do business with a firm they think is needy or hungry. When setting a meeting time with a client or prospect, don't say, "Any time next week would be fine." You give the impression that you have nothing to do. Instead, provide several time/date choices.

Reprinted with permission of Jean Shenson.

HOW DAVID CAN BEAT GOLIATH

Small firms can win big business against the Goliaths by following the giants' example, suggests Ward White, former colleague, former President Golin/Harris-East and now Vice President, Communications, Northwestern Mutual Life Insurance, Milwaukee, WI (and a top-notch new business proposal writer to boot). In a speech to the Public Relations Society of America Counselors Academy Spring Conference, White recommended:

1. Recognize that the giants use sound strategies in their new business efforts. Big firms have good, smart people who are good strategists. They respond to what the customer wants.
2. Recognize that it's a changing world. No practitioner can keep doing the same old tricks. There are new strategies . . . old strategies with new tricks . . . and they are used because they work.
3. The expert is the guy from out of town. Goliath may bring bodies from each of the prospect's markets or people who have worked in his business. You can combat this by making sure you get very smart about the prospect's company, industry and markets.
4. Nobody wants to hire a generalist. Clients want to hire a specialist, someone who can speak their secret language, someone who knows their markets even better than they do and who can teach them new things.
5. You can't fake it anymore. Today's market demands legitimate specialization and genuine expertise, either geographic or industry-specific. If you don't have the in-depth experience, you have to go out and get it . . . any way you can . . . through alliances, sub-contracts, contingency hires.
6. Become a specialist . . . in many areas. In truth, you are a specialist in each of the areas you've worked. Go modular in your brochure and presentation. A multi-purpose, one-size-fits-all capabilities brochure . . . because it lists all your specialties . . . is not credible.
   Your general brochure can be very general: what you believe in, your technology, your commitment to service, your systems. However, also produce companion pieces, with the same look, on each of your specialties. If you use a slide show, talk only about relevant clients. Resist the temptation to showcase every talent. Customize videos.
7. Research sells. It's extremely powerful to fascinate the prospect with something new. There are lots of ways to gather information: survey trade editors, the metro press, consultants, analysts, customers. Clients want a firm that not only understands their business but also knows their customers.

Read annual reports, security analyst research reports, sales literature, and, especially, work the data bases. (Compu-Serve, for example, provides access to broad demographic data including household profiles, reader/viewer habits and business patterns.) If you don't have a staff member who knows how to access data bases, hire an external researcher or, perhaps, a college professor or computer specialist.

8. Strategy sells; PR tactics don't. Prospects are not interested in how you're going to get the job done; they're interested that you understand the job that needs to be done.

9. Don't be tempted to over-promise. (Even though others may.) Emphasize that your style is to under-promise and over-deliver.

10. Don't be worried about a lack of international offices. Almost nobody ever uses them. Arrange to put dots on a map through a network or loose affiliation and concentrate on your home market or specialty market niche.

11. Emphasize details such as proofreading. If you make a mistake, don't call attention to it.

12. Emphasize thoroughness and reliability.

13. Keep in touch with lost prospects. When the honeymoon is over, in three to six months, you may be in a good position to pick up the once-lost business.

14. Don't shoot yourself in the foot. Don't take unnecessary chances. Forget that really-off-the-wall creative brainstorm. Stick with sound fundamentals, especially if you're the favorite.

15. Business people cannot read. Make things clear and simple. Use bullet-dot phrases. Elliptical sentences. Pare it down to the bone. Eliminate words. Explain all you want orally . . . just don't put it in the written pitch.

16. No Chinese menus. Be very specific on proposed program budget costs.

17. K.I.S.S. (Keep It Simple, Stupid.) Talk a lot about your research. But use discipline on objectives and strategies; only three or four of each. Keep recommendations simple. Leave out the details.

Summary: Think like a prospect; get inside the prospect's head. Put the prospect's interests first. Live his or her problem. Bring to bear whatever resources are needed, inside or outside your firm. Present a solution and you have a client.

Reprinted with permission of Ward White, Vice President, Communications, Northwestern Mutual Life Insurance Company.

Side note: If you take White's advice, you are sure to beat Goliath every time. Well, almost every time.

SEVEN SECRETS TO SELL SERVICE

Jim Lukaszewski, Chairman, The Lukaszewski Group, White Plains, NY recommends:

1. Structure and update. Ask "Has anything changed since we last spoke?" Often, there are critical changes between the time you receive the proposal request and first talk to the prospect and the presentation itself. Being first to present puts you at a disadvantage because each succeeding firm has more information on which to base their presentation as the prospect more clearly perceives his or her real needs.
2. Recommend ideas, concepts, goals and tactics. Deal as quickly as possible with the ways in which your firm would handle the assignment. Agencies often waste prospects' time with nonpertinent information, such as administrative procedures and current clients, because either they are afraid of having their ideas stolen or they don't have any substantive ideas and are hopeful that one or two will surface from the prospect during the presentation.
3. Organize your proposal with your prospect's goals in mind. Address first your prospect's most critical need. Agencies often spend too much time talking about rudimentary tactics such as news releases, media contact, etc. If your ideas about how the prospect should handle his most important issue are appropriate, the technical details will take care of themselves.
4. Leverage off the prospect's existing experience and resources. Recognize how much energy and talent the prospect can pro-

vide by clarifying the most valuable augmenting services that you will provide. Prospects are usually more interested in the ideas, concepts and criticism that they cannot generate internally than having you take over their entire communications effort.

5. Reveal key parts of your research early in the presentation. Share your strategy. Don't hold a good idea until the end of the presentation or be afraid to share it. Presentations are won on the basis of chemistry between individuals and the ideas shared. Ask for the prospect's reaction to your approach.

6. Sell your unique capability to do this job. Too often, agencies spend all their time talking about their ability to do many things. The prospect cares only about how you can bring credible help to the problem at hand.

7. Focus on closing the sale. Go for the "Magic Two Minutes," the time in every selling situation when the time is right to close the sale. Three tips to move to the Magic Two Minutes: (1) Be enthusiastic about doing the work; (2) Talk in terms of positive, specific, meaningful project outcomes; and (3) Ask for the order by asking the prospect to hire you.

© James E. Lukaszewski. Reprinted with permission.

GAIN A COMPETITIVE EDGE THROUGH DATA BASE ACCESS

You can gain a competitive edge by accessing electronic data bases to learn more about prospects, their markets and industries. In addition to gaining information about prospects, you can use on-line data bases as both a selling and measurement tool.

Look in one of the data bases, such as *The New York Times*, for mentions of the prospect's name in publications included in the data base. At the same time, look for mentions of two or three of the prospect's biggest competitors.

On a data printout, mark each company with a different color. For example, in the past year, the prospect had 18 mentions; competitors A, B and C had 22, 16 and 27 mentions respectively. Use the printout during the presentation to show the prospect, in a dramatic fashion, how his company is lagging behind its competitors in valuable media coverage. (Obviously, this technique only works if your prospect has fewer published mentions than his competitors.) It drives prospects crazy to see that their competitors have more colored marks on the printout than they do.

As a measurement device, set a realistic goal to increase the number of mentions of the client in the same data base by the end of the first year. At the end of the year, show the now-client how his media coverage improved compared to competitors after he hired your firm.

There are two ways to use on-line electronic research services: (1) Hire an outside research service to search for information on prospect operations, markets and industry trends. The cost should be about $75-$100 per hour. (2) Hook a modem to your computer system, sign up for one or more of the on-line research services–such as America Online or CompuServ–and search data bases yourself. If you don't subscribe to at least one such on-line service, you are trailing behind the two-thirds of agencies who do.

Warning: Restrict use of such services. On-line data base searches can be time-consuming and costly unless you know precisely what you're looking for and how to find it. Suggestion: Train one person on your staff to conduct such research. A California PR firm estimated it cut annual costs by $3,500 by eliminating outside research and training an administrative staff member to conduct data searches.

This is only a faint dusting of the information available in books and magazines about electronic research services and on-line data bases. Consult your local library or friendly computer guru for more complete information.

QUESTIONS TO ASK PROSPECTS

Here (from the late Howard Shenson's *Shenson on Consulting– Success Strategies From the Consultant's Consultant*) are some questions you may want to ask during your first meeting with a prospect. They will help get to the heart of his or her needs. (Remember, most new business is won . . . or lost . . . during your first meeting with the prospect.)

1. What is the major problem your organization faces?
2. What problems do you face that are shared by the rest of the industry or similar organizations?
3. What problems confront your organization that are unique to this geographic area?
4. Has inadequate planning contributed to the problems facing your organization? How?
5. Have government regulations affected the profitability of your organization? How?
6. How does your organization rank in the industry in terms of salary, benefits, employee perks?
7. If your organization is family owned, to what extent does this ownership affect promotions and employee morale?
8. What kind of staff turnover do you have? Is this trend up or down from previous years?
9. Have you made any changes in personnel policy based on your assessments of employee satisfaction and productivity?
10. How long have your key management and technical people been with your organization?
11. How far in advance do you make specific decisions about expansion?
12. What has been your most disappointing area of growth over the past two years?
13. In what ways do you ensure that expenditures on training will produce the desired results?
14. How do communications work within your organization?
15. How do you identify communication breakdowns in the organization?
16. Who reports to whom in your organization?
17. What is the biggest time bomb in your organization? What steps have been taken, or do you plan to take, to deal with this problem?
18. What impact do you see company problems having on management and staff?
19. What new products or services do you see as vital within the next ten years for your organization to maintain or increase its growth?

"Don't ask questions for which you already have answers," Shenson said. "Don't waste the prospect's time. If you can't think of something new, creative and interesting to ask, you probably shouldn't be talking to the prospect in the first place."

The prospect will also likely ask you a series of questions. In addition, Shenson suggests, he or she may have other questions on their minds . . . that they may not ask. However, Shenson recommends that you win points by answering questions such as these before or whether they are asked:

1. Do I need this service?
2. Do I really want this service?
3. Can I really afford this service?
4. Will I make use of the knowledge I gain? How?
5. Am I being given a good idea?
6. Should I check out the competition?
7. Could I get this service for less?
8. Is this firm professional, honest, knowledgeable and reliable?
9. Should I decide now or later?
10. What will my colleagues thing?
11. What problems may result if I don't act now?"

Reprinted with permission from Jean Shenson.

THE KILLER QUESTIONS THAT PROSPECTS ASK

You're trying to win the big one: an RFP shoot-out against four or five other agencies for a major piece of business (in which you had to pull out all the stops just to make the short list); or an exclusive audience with the CEO of a desirable prospect you've been courting for a long time.

You rehearsed your pitch well and delivered it with gusto. Now it's time for questions. And the prospect hits you with a meat ax . . . the very questions you hoped you wouldn't hear.

Jim Lukaszewski, chairman, The Lukaszewski Group, White Plains, NY, suggests that there are Seven Killer Questions that you should anticipate, be ready for, and even head off.

"Killer questions don't surprise you," said Lukaszewski. "They irritate you. When you hear them you get a clung–an adrenaline shot that rips through your body and melts your guts like cream cheese down into your shoes.

"What's the answer? Be ready, perhaps even bring up these questions yourself and answer them to save the prospect the potential embarrassment of having to ask them, hurt your feelings or seem impolite. Clients have a right to the answers; you have the obligation to be prepared."

Lukaszewski's Seven Killer Questions:

1. Have you ever done this before?
   More (prospects) than ever before are asking this question . . . directly," Lukaszewski said.
   Prospective clients assume that you would not have allowed yourself ethically to be in the presentation without disclosing this up front. The prospect has a right to know this and to deliberately have you make a presentation knowing you don't have the experience or background for the work.
2. Who else have you done it for?
   Logically, if your answer to Number 1 is "Yes," the prospect is going to want to know who, how, when and, most importantly, the results. This is the time when agencies like to waffle and say something like, "Well . . . not exactly, but we worked for XYZ Corporation doing something somewhat similar." Obviously, this answer is not a prospect confidence builder. [Try to present] relevant examples, develop scenarios you can achieve.
3. What if it doesn't work?
   So what? This is a problem if you only have one idea. This is like the fear of being asked a question about a narrow idea that the prospect may already have rejected. The answer is to always have a "Plan B," even a "Plan C" or "Plan D." Be prepared for the unanticipated consequence of an unsuccessful effort. And you'll be able to better talk about that in the presentation.
4. Why should we select you?
   [Some years ago, Ted Kennedy, running for president, was asked by a national news anchor why he was running. Kennedy said it was a very interesting question, but he really had not

thought about it. This is one of those kind of questions.] Why do you want this particular work? There must be some unique reasons why your agency is particularly appropriate for the work you're pitching. What are the two or three most important reasons, from the prospect's perspective, that they ought to hire you?

[Hint]: Prospects like to hear: specific experience; unusually direct experience; creative approaches; and clear and direct solutions.

5. Why should we hire you rather than XYZ agency?

It isn't necessary to know your competition thoroughly. [Side note: We happen to disagree strongly with Jim on this point, but that's another story.] However, you ought to look around your marketplace and, perhaps, pick a very large agency, a medium-size agency and a very small agency and determine why you should be hired instead of them. There is no reason to be unprepared to respond to this kind of comparative question. Your answer should reflect the insight, perception and doability the prospect is looking for. If you can't answer the question, you may not have the other skills the prospect needs either.

Warning: Stick to the positives. Prospects are reluctant to purchase on negative sales points. If you cut apart another agency's talents, capabilities or track record, it's likely that neither you nor (the other agency) will win. Clients want creativity without conflict.

6. What are your weaknesses?

Prospects ask this question because they've been burned. They are used to having agencies say they can do just about anything. Surely, your firm does not do everything. It may be an important credibility builder to talk (briefly and unapologetically) about the two or three things that your agency does not do.

Caution: Clients will clearly and very directly remember what you do not do once you have told them. While disclaiming certain skills and abilities will build your credibility, it also may foreclose you from ever doing that kind of work for the client . . . unless you can reeducate him or her once you've achieved these new capabilities. The secret is to have consultants or other firms on tap to handle areas in which you are weak.

7. Will you teach our people what you know?

[Side note: In 25 years in the agency business, I never heard this one. Evidently Lukaszewski has.]

Your answer should always be an absolute and enthusiastic "Yes." Never be threatened by teaching your clients what you know. Clients hire agencies because agencies have unique skills that most corporate and other organizations simply are never able to capture or build. If you can teach a client what you know and they can turn around and do it . . . you don't deserve to continue the relationship unless you find another way to build value into your services beyond the level at which the client was able to take over.

© James E. Lukaszewski. Reprinted with permission.

TEN WAYS TO RUIN A NEW BUSINESS PRESENTATION

Unfortunately, no matter how good your initial chemistry with the prospect was; no matter how thorough your research was; no matter how well written your "leave" document is . . . a clumsy oral presentation can sink you and lose the business.

Here . . . based on experience and talks with firm principals and corporate PR executives . . . are ten ways that you can lose the business during the final presentation:

1. Be Arrogant

One of the two biggest mistakes you can make is to alienate prospects by "preaching" to them or insulting them by implying that their PR program is not effective or that their PR director has not been doing his or her job effectively. You can also turn off the prospect by putting down his current PR firm or your competition.

2. Be Uninformed

This is the second biggest mistake. Misread, ignore or never learn what the prospect expects from the presentation; what type of presentation he/she/committee would be most comfortable with; what kind of pitch would best match the prospect's corporate culture. Do a "dog and pony" show when a casual across-the-table dialogue would have been more suitable. Or play it ultra-casual when the prospect would have been impressed by more "glitz." Use too few/too many or overly elaborate visuals. Fail to consider the type of presentations competing firms will make.

3. Be Ignorant

Tell offensive, racist, chauvinistic jokes. Use profanity. Ignore the "little people" on the prospect committee. Talk only to the most senior person . . . who may approve the agency choice, but not make the initial selection. Avoid learning the titles and job responsibilities of all review committee members.

4. Be Windy

Do all the talking. (One agency head recommends that firms spend 30 percent of the time talking and 70 percent listening.) Try to cover too much in the time allotted. Forget about limiting your presentation to what the prospect really wants to hear. Don't leave time for prospect questions. Go over the time deadline.

5. Be Expensive

Confirm what the prospect has heard or believes: "PR firms are expensive." Scare him/her by talking about all the big budget clients you have. Be too "showy"; use elaborate visuals or creative effects that look like they cost a lot of money. Recommend primarily big, obviously-expensive projects.

6. Be Superfluous

Bring too many people into the presentation. Include staff members who have no role in the presentation. Let one agency executive dominate the discussion. Don't involve practitioners who will actually serve the prospect's business.

7. Be Phony

Try to make the prospect believe that your firm or people are something that they are not. Don't stay within your own comfort range; maybe you can convince the prospect that you are what he's looking for . . . even if you're not sure what that is.

Sell too hard. Appear desperate for the business. Forget human relations values and caveats. Don't worry about chemistry; who knows what that is, anyway? If all else fails, offer the prospect a kickback; theater, football or baseball tickets are always nice.

8. Be Invisible

Forget that the prospect may have sat through three to six other presentations (perhaps, back to back). Don't worry about building something creative and unique into your presentation that will distinguish your firm from all the others in the competition. Also forget about being enthusiastic; don't show interest and the desire to be involved with the prospect. When you say "we," make sure the prospect understands that you mean only the agency . . . not the agency and the prospect/client.

Drone your way through a boring, canned presentation without lifting your eyes from the script. Don't try to present either first or last, rather than in the middle of a series of competitive presentations. After lunch is a great time to make a presentation, right?

And, by all means, never follow up your presentation with a thank-you note or a broader answer to one of the prospect's questions.

9. Be Noncompetitive

Don't worry about competing firms. Ride on your reputation; no need for a 150 percent effort in the presentation. This one is locked up; you're the biggest firm in town or the prospect's PR director formerly worked for your firm or is a good friend. [Side note: Many firms would rather lose the business than have a former employee as a client.]

10. Be Disorganized

Don't visit the presentation site in advance to check out ambiance, size, acoustics, or the seating arrangement. Don't set up or rearrange the presentation room (if in the prospect's quarters) for good eye and personal contact between the prospect and agency people. Arrive at the last minute so there's little time or opportunity to set up your equipment or make room changes.

Don't make sure needed audio visual equipment will be available. Forget to bring extension cords, electric plugs, masking tape, marking pens, flip charts and easels, name tent cards and other equipment.

Don't bother checking whether your slide tray will fit the prospect's projector and the prospect's videotape player will accept your tape. And don't worry about whether the cap is tight on your slide tray and the slides are in order.

Don't rehearse your presentation. Forget about making sure that people know exactly what they are supposed to do . . . and are comfortable with their assignment. Don't coach neophyte presenters or give them plenty of time to rehearse. Don't "role play" answers to questions the prospect may ask or decide who will answer questions. Don't ask uninvolved agency people to critique your rehearsal; ignore their comments, if you do. Don't arrange for the presentation to be in your quarters or invite the prospect for a get-acquainted visit. If the presentation is on your turf, don't give the prospect an agency tour to provide a feel for your agency atmosphere and facilities. All agencies look alike, right? Don't clean up messy offices or make sure there aren't too many unoccupied, obviously unused offices. All agencies have cluttered halls and stacks of press kits piled in the corner of the conference room, don't they?

When the prospect accepts your invitation to lunch in your conference room before the presentation, make sure that he's the only one who eats. (A corporate PR executive described his discomfort when a major firm pulled this one on him.)

Don't place a welcoming sign in your reception area or prepare any prominent visuals or displays that relate to the prospect or his business.

Making one of these mistakes may not kill you. Two mistakes and you still might squeak through. (Maybe the prospect's PR director really is your best friend or cousin.) But why take chances? Reverse the polarity of these ten ways to ruin a good presentation . . . and the big ones won't get away.

MISTAKES THAT PROSPECTS MAKE

Here are 11 common mistakes that prospects make during an agency search. By subtly alerting prospects to these potential mistakes, you will help assure that they pick the right firm. Hopefully, it will be yours.

1. Does not meet personally with firms; will not permit firms to speak to company executives beyond the PR director;
2. Does not provide realistic budget parameters; describes bigger budget than available;
3. Is not candid/comprehensive about the company background/reputation/problems/opportunities;
4. Searches for free ideas, not an agency (maybe never picks a firm);
5. Seeks competitive pitches when a new firm has already been selected . . . but not announced;
6. Does not define/provide PR/corporate objectives;
7. Does not define type of presentation expected;
8. Demands extensive, free, speculative recommendations;
9. Will not disclose names of competing firms;
10. Interviews too many firms; and
11. Does not understand the difference between advertising and PR and what each can/cannot accomplish.

PROFILE 8

JACK GUTHRIE, CHAIRMAN, JACK GUTHRIE & ASSOCIATES, LOUISVILLE, KY

Talk about long-range planning! Guthrie conceived the idea for starting his PR firm in 1969 when there were no others in town. While his plan called for opening the doors in 1974, a recession delayed the big event until 1977. By then, he had competition; one other firm. By then, he had also amassed exceptionally strong local contacts and support. Guthrie's background includes eight years in PR with Philip Morris USA in New York and Louisville, and six years as Executive Vice President, Chief Executive Officer of the famed Kentucky Derby Festival.

Jack Guthrie & Associates has grown from $175,000 income the first year to about $1.5 million and is the largest independent firm in Kentucky. Start-up clients included Philip Morris, Liberty National Bank, Glenmore Distillers, and the Louisville Airport. Prime clients today also include Toyota Motor Manufacturing USA and United Parcel Service.

Despite his long-range plan, Guthrie found that start-up costs were twice what he'd expected and that local, state and Federal paperwork was overwhelming. He claims three employees at start-up ("Me, myself and I–each working eight-hour shifts seven days a week") compared to 21 real employees now.

For new principals, Guthrie advises: "Review budget projections carefully, then add at least 50 percent; make sure your equipment including computers is state of the art; and hire experienced people, if at all possible."

Chapter 8

New Business Singular Truths

While competing for and winning–or losing–new clients, you will recognize a few singular truths. These truths should provide the critical core of your new business development campaign.

TRUTH NO. 1: THE FIRST ENCOUNTER WITH A PROSPECT IS CRITICAL

Chances are you already know that first impressions are very important. When it comes to new business solicitation, the first impression–your very first meeting with a prospect–is so important that it can make the difference between whether you win or lose a piece of new business.

The impression that you make in your first meeting with a prospect can overcome the organized frenzy of a series of formal presentations where prospects may have trouble remembering the difference between competing agencies. In many instances, the first meeting will determine whether you make the "short list" and are invited into the final presentation round.

The first meeting or prospect briefing is an opportunity for you to dig into the prospect's background and needs and establish direction for your formal presentation. It is also an opportunity for the prospect to preview your firm's experience, eagerness and intuitiveness in an unfettered, unstructured atmosphere. Here's an example from real life.

I was retained by a well-known national corporation to assist in the selection of a new public relations firm. Six PR agencies were invited to receive separate briefings from a corporate committee that included senior executives. One of the firms, actually the PR department of the company's advertising agency, declined the briefing on the basis that they already knew enough about the company. Said they didn't need to waste the company's time. (Too bad! The firm bombed its presentation.)

The other five firms spent at least an hour each (some more) with the prospect's committee. I soon became aware that the committee was very impressed with the representatives of a national firm. Two senior officers of the firm had come into the briefing meeting well prepared. They had obviously researched the company and had even visited one of the company's retail outlets. They asked intelligent questions and made pertinent comments and suggestions.

On the morning of the first presentation–with six scheduled over two days–the committee assembled early to review the agency screening procedure. As they left to visit the first agency, the CEO moaned, "Why are we going through this? We know who we're going to pick."

And they did. The firm whose representatives had come into the first meeting smart enough about the company to ask intelligent questions won the business. And still has it at this writing ten years later.

I saw this pattern many times over a period of years as I helped companies conduct agency searches. In the middle of the search process, a PR director would say, "We really like XYZ Agency." And, generally, that would be the firm that they chose.

Ok, so I'll repeat myself. Don't waste your time and that of your prospect–don't insult your prospect–by going into the first meeting unprepared. Run a data base check. Talk to a couple of editors. Read a trade publication or two. Visit a trade show. Use the product. Invest enough time to learn the prospect's business so you can look smarter–can be smarter–than your competitors.

TRUTH NO. 2: A PROSPECT'S AGENDA MAY NOT BE AS IT SEEMS

Often, the prospect's needs, as he or she expresses them, may seem relatively uncomplicated and unsophisticated, centered largely on publicity and "big ideas."

However, be careful. Lurking behind such simplistic goals often is an unrecognized but nascent need for trend tracking, problem anticipation, strategic thinking, corporate or marketing positioning and professional direction.

Depending on the sophistication of the prospect, he may not even be aware of the breadth of services he can receive from your firm. Probing the client's problems and opportunities during an initial meeting could lead to a broader–and more profitable–program than initially envisioned.

TRUTH NO. 3: THE IMPORTANCE OF CULTURE COMPATIBILITY CANNOT BE OVERESTIMATED

Culture compatibility, comfort fit or "chemistry" between agency and prospect is often hard to discern or define and frequently relies on gut feelings. However, it can be the deciding factor in an agency search and one of the most important elements in a productive ongoing agency-client relationship.

Corporate or agency culture wears many cloaks; it can be billed as historical heritage . . . inherited interests, instincts and ethos . . . personality profile or, as *Webster's New World Dictionary* sees it, "The sum total of ways of living built up by a group of human beings and transmitted from one generation to another."

However defined, culture is the essence of corporate and agency flavor, drive and direction. It is a given; established and nurtured over a lengthy period of time and not subject to transient variations to fit individual situations.

A lack of culture compatibility between agency and prospect should not be judged as "good" or "bad," but only in terms of "vive la différence." Where culture compatibility does not exist in one instance, it will flourish in another. Not all clients and agencies were meant to live happily ever after. Recognizing the potential for such compatibility at an early stage is one of the prime virtues and hoped-for outcomes of your first exploratory meeting with a prospect.

WHY AGENCIES WIN OR LOSE NEW BUSINESS

In a survey of agency principals, chemistry, good fit and industry experience were almost unanimously listed as reasons why agencies win or lose new business. Other reasons for winning business listed by survey respondents included:

- We do our homework. We are perceived as genuine down-to-earth people who care about and invest a lot of passion and energy in our clients' success.
- We are viewed as "superb" at both strategy and execution.
- Personal reputation and recognized expertise in certain areas.
- Prestige of existing clients.
- Good value.
- Straightforward plan.
- We make a point of being in the right place at the right time. That usually means being there first. We do a lot of homework on prospects. Our pitches are more strategic than cosmetic.
- Listening to the prospect.
- Breadth of services.
- Aggressive attitude and quality presentations; and
- Assurance of quality and quantity of work at better prices.

In addition to a lack of chemistry, firm principals said they don't win business because:

- Clients who value one activity above all else might choose a firm that is good at that activity.
- Small size.
- Price.
- The prospect doesn't realize that the agency is a business that needs to make money.
- Pre-ordained outcome.
- No budget after all.
- Lack of experience (in a specific industry).
- The prospect doesn't understand or accept (the value) of our comprehensive services when we're pitching against a narrow specialist.
- Location.
- Client goes with a "safe," better-known agency.
- Unable to convince prospect of benefits.
- Larger agency strongly recommended by prestigious friend of CEO or board member; and

- Prospect doesn't understand PR or our strengths. (From experience helping corporations choose a PR firm, I know that one very strong reason why firms fail to win a new client–a reason that companies seldom mention–is the firms' emphasis on functional recommendations–tactics and techniques–rather than on solid strategies supporting the prospects' corporate or marketing objectives.)

Good "chemistry" depends heavily on strategically strong thinking that will help prospects meet their goals.

TRUTH NO. 4: PROSPECTS' PRIORITIES ARE SELDOM THE SAME AS YOURS

You're squirming, impatient, apprehensive. At the end of your pitch last week to a gargantuan prospect, the PR director promised to make an agency selection by the end of this week. It's Friday, but you haven't heard anything yet. You're convinced that you lost. The atmosphere tends to be gloomy and you spend the weekend sulking and barking at your wife, husband, children or dog.

Not to fret. Prospects' priorities are seldom the same as yours. They'll get around to it when they get around to it.

I've seen instances where the agency pitched last out of six firms, left to return to its office and was called back in and awarded the business on the spot. I've seen other instances where a promised quick decision stretched out to several months and sometimes to never.

Agencies often ask, "When do you expect to make your decision?" It's probably a useless question. Circumstances or events that you know nothing about–because you are not yet privy to the company's secrets–can delay agency selection decisions for a lot longer than you would like.

A couple of generalities: Consumer product companies usually make decisions quicker than industrial companies. However, industrial companies who may take forever to decide to hire a PR firm will usually take equally as long to decide to fire one. The same may not be true of consumer companies.

Selecting a new PR agency may not be a high priority with the prospect, compared to other company problems. And you can't make it happen any faster even if the cold wind is blowing at your door and your cash flow chart is bleeding.

Your best bet is to make your presentation; follow up with a brief thank-you letter and then pretend the presentation never happened. Go about your business. This way, you'll be pleasantly surprised when the prospect calls with the good news that you won. And if you didn't win, well, there's always that great prospect you're pitching next week.

TRUTH NO. 5: YOU MUST BE ABLE TO ACCEPT AND BOUNCE BACK FROM REJECTION

During my early years in the agency business, a colleague asked, "How can you get up off the floor so often?" (He later left for a corporate job.) I thought, "Why not? I don't like it down there. There are splinters and the dirt gets under my fingernails. Besides, I'm having fun. I can't help it if the prospect is not perceptive or wise enough to choose us."

The truth is, every salesman must learn to accept and live with rejection, and not take it personally. As the principal of your agency, that's what you are, a salesman. If you don't get up off the floor after being knocked down, the only sounds you'll hear are the footsteps of your competitors running over you and the bank knocking on your door.

You must get up and wage the battle. Again. And again. And again. That is the only answer.

TRUTH NO. 6: BE PATIENT— WINNING NEW CLIENTS TAKES TIME

That says it all. Good luck.

PART III.
MANAGING YOUR FIRM
FOR PROFIT

PROFILE 9

ELIZABETH HAYS, CEO, DAVIS, HAYS & COMPANY, MAYWOOD, NJ

When *Nation's Business* interviewed Hays in early 1993 for its "Entrepreneur's Notebook," Davis, Hays & Company was one of the fastest growing firms in the PR industry. In the ten years since Hays and partner Alison Davis started their agency income has grown to just under $1 million. Their client list includes such well-known names as Hoffmann-La Roche, Booz, Allen & Hamilton, and Consolidated Edison of New York. But the rule book says it probably should not have happened.

As Hays noted, "To grow, we substituted common sense and a few contrarian practices for entrepreneurial experience." The partners virtually ignored the down economy and concentrated on planning for success. Rather than try to do everything themselves, they hired staff "for the future" so they could focus on improving the business. Rather than penny-pinch, they invested heavily in technology. And they weren't afraid to resign unprofitable accounts.

The partners also recognized that marketing was critical. "Like dieting, it works but only when you do it," Hays says. The firm was an early user of a telemarketer to qualify prospects and arrange appointments for the partners.

Now, the partners are concentrating on following a realistic business plan with attention to the firm's bottom line. "One of our strategies is managed growth. However, we're not out to build an empire. We all have other interests and relationships that are important to us," Hays says.

Chapter 9

Management Strategies for Success

Every successful public relations firm principal walks a narrow tight rope. You must adroitly manage dual–and potentially conflicting–responsibilities. You must ensure that your firm provides the best possible client service. To accomplish this, you must manage, monitor and/or participate in current client assignments. Simultaneously, you must protect and advance your bottom line by controlling costs, encouraging high staff productivity and taking every opportunity to increase income and profits from current and new clients.

Assiduously following the track laid down by the following ten management strategies will help ensure that these dual responsibilities are fulfilled and that the potential conflict is managed in a win-win fashion.

DEVELOP A PRACTICAL LONG-RANGE BUSINESS PLAN

If you have not already done so, develop a long-range business plan to provide a direction for your future growth and a benchmark to measure your success. If you already have a plan, review it carefully and critically to make sure that it still fits your firm and accommodates changes in your firm's structure, goals or markets. Then work the plan.

Your business plan should extend at least three to five years and should include such ingredients as:

- a description of your firm;
- an analysis of your market;

- a portrait of your competition;
- an overview of current and planned services;
- a marketing and sales plan;
- a personnel profile; and
- a pro-forma financial statement.

Don't write the plan and abandon it in a file folder. Refer to it regularly as a meaningful guide for your daily activities and as a perpetual reminder of your goals.

Update the plan at least annually. Incorporate changes in your organization; note additional current or potential markets; add, delete or change the description of your competition; add new services you provide or delete those that you no longer offer; update the description of your personnel, noting staff strengths and weaknesses and the type of personnel you may need in the future; revise your marketing plan to promote new services or reach new objectives; and project a realistic view of your firm's financial potential.

Analyze those aspects of your plan that have been productive and look for ways to strengthen them. Eliminate parts of the plan that have proven to be impractical or unrealistic.

Invite your key senior people to help develop or revise the plan. Involve your total staff in the success of your firm; make sure that everyone understands and supports your goals for the firm, the direction the firm is taking, the obstacles you face and the part they play in overcoming the obstacles and achieving firm goals. Be sure that everyone understands and appreciates what achieving these goals can mean to their own personal growth and security. Invite all employees to an annual "job holders" meeting to review the past year's progress and the next year's potential candidly and in detail.

ESTABLISH REASONABLE REALISTIC GROWTH GOALS

Do you want to run a small, profitable firm where you can retain substantial hands-on contact with clients or build a larger firm where your management skills will be as valuable or even more valuable than your professional public relations skills? Decide if, how, and in what direction you want your firm to grow. Project both profit and income goals. Growth goals of 15 to 20 percent annually are reasonable and realistic.

Be sure to write your goals down. Research indicates that spelling out goals in writing helps ensure their achievement.

DEVELOP A STRATEGIC POSITION OR MARKET NICHE

Public relations industry pundits foretell a future in which there are a few large firms with global capabilities and a large number of successful small- and medium-size firms serving local and regional needs and special market niches. Unless you realistically expect to expand globally, pick your target market(s) early on and concentrate your efforts on achieving recognition and success in those markets. However, be alert for opportunities and flexible enough to move quickly into new areas or phase out of markets that are drying up.

As part of your business plan, develop a strategic position for your firm. Describe what your firm is; what you want it to be; the kind of clients you want; and the markets you currently serve and those that offer opportunities.

Analyze your current capabilities and those you'll need to move into opportunity markets. Delineate your strengths and corporate culture, the things that make your firm unique and memorable. Explore steps you can take to ensure that clients and prospects perceive your firm in step with reality. Community perception of your firm may lag as much as two years behind reality.

Ask your staff members to write a short description of your firm's unique characteristics and position, as they see them, or throw out the question during a staff meeting. Compare their appraisal with your own. Make sure all your employees can describe your firm in a similar manner. And consider asking your clients to describe the way they see your firm.

Write a 25-word description of your firm's strategic position and post it on your bulletin board. Decide what you will say when a prospect asks you to tell him or her the most significant thing about your firm . . . the thing that sets your firm apart from competition and is most important to your clients.

Promote your firm's strategic position and make sure that everything you do aligns with, supports or strengthens that position.

CONDUCT AN ONGOING MARKETING PROGRAM

Do for your firm what you do for your clients. Budget for and conduct an ongoing self-marketing program that includes such elements as publicity, literature, direct mail and personal contact. See Chapter 4 for detailed self-marketing recommendations.

ESTABLISH A REPUTATION FOR CREATIVITY, STRATEGIC SAVVY AND MEANINGFUL RESULTS

Companies looking for a new public relations firm usually base their decision largely on three factors: personal chemistry or the culture compatibility between the prospect and the firm; the firm's strength in strategically driven creativity; and its ability to produce and demonstrate meaningful results.

Creativity tied to strong corporate or marketing strategies will win the prospect every day. "Big Ideas" or special events that do little more than generate unfocused media attention pale in comparison to a unique creative approach supporting a tight, targeted strategy. And more and more companies demand the latter.

In addition, clients increasingly refuse to put much value on or accept results whose only evidence is a book of clippings and a cassette of TV news clips. Instead, progressive public relations firms have developed an expanding array of techniques to measure and evaluate both "process or input" results (measured in terms of the total media impressions generated in support of specific objectives) and "outcome or impact" results (measured in terms of public changes in awareness, attitudes and behavior).

Successful firms continually and persuasively merchandise their strengths in strategically-driven creativity as well as their ability to produce meaningful results that demonstrate the client's return on investment.

One excellent way to merchandise your strategic, creative and result capabilities is to enter your best campaigns in local and national professional competitions. However, entering a competition deserves a full commitment of time and effort to ensure that your entry properly documents the details and success of the program. Any lesser, last-minute effort is a waste of time and money.

ENCOURAGE AND ENSURE HIGH STAFF PRODUCTIVITY

One of the most common problems encountered by small- and medium-size firms in particular is low productivity; i.e., staff members billing less than an average of 85 percent of their time to clients. Low productivity can result from a number of factors including:

- Poor management planning;
- Faulty resource allocation;
- Over-staffing;
- Lack of enough business;
- Well-meaning but over-zealous management intentions to create good working conditions; and
- Poor employee motivation.

It is not uncommon for a firm's average productivity to sink as low as 60 percent. Consider that, at only 60 percent billable, a single account executive billing at $90 per hour can cost your firm more than $30,000 in lost income annually.

Assuring firm-wide high productivity, of course, requires that enough work is available on a continuing basis to keep people busy and that efforts are made to smooth out the cyclical nature of the agency business.

An ongoing marketing campaign (especially important when you are the busiest), proper and practical anticipation of client needs and allocating work loads across all employees can do much to ensure high productivity.

However, consistent high productivity depends most critically on establishing and maintaining excellent staff morale and motivation. Employees need to understand, be recognized for and be proud of their contribution to your firm's success. They need to develop a strong sense of their own self-worth. And they need to be trained and encouraged to anticipate high and low work loads and to balance their own productivity by getting help in handling peak loads or asking for additional work when their own client load is about to drop off. A high level of staff interdependence is essential to overall high productivity.

Based on a seven-hour day, staff members can be expected to bill, on the average, about 1,200 hours a year to clients. For planning purposes, use the conservative averages of 1,300 hours annually for a seven and one-half hour day and 1,400 hours for an eight-hour day. The average per-professional annual income potential is about $130,000.

Staff members will appreciate knowing their worth to the firm and they need to understand and support your productivity expectations. Anything less than an average 80-85 percent productivity across the board means your income and profit are less than they could and should be.

TRACK INDIVIDUAL CLIENT PROFITABILITY

To assure overall profitability, you must be able to track and control the profitability of individual clients. You need to be aware of and able to root out profit leaks. If you don't already have such a system, ask your accountant to set one up.

Most systems that track client profitability involve two major factors: the salary-cost-to-income ratio for each client; and a standard percentage share of firm overhead assigned to each client. Depending on client needs, you can control individual client profitability by adjusting the salary cost ratio. The lower the salary-to-income ratio percentage, the higher your profits will be. Ratios below 30-33 percent will ensure good profitability. The Golden Rule (Golden as in "dollars"), of course, is to ensure that, while maintaining excellent client service, the most highly qualified, least costly staff members do most of the work.

Flat fees, though comforting from a cash flow standpoint, can quickly and easily be unprofitable. If you can't make an account profitable, consider resigning the client!

CHARGE A FAIR AND ADEQUATE PRICE
FOR YOUR SERVICES

Public relations firms are forbidden by law to discuss or exchange information on the hourly rates that they charge in any way that could be construed as price fixing. The reality is that most firms have a pretty good idea of prevailing rates in their area. And the fact is that you don't do yourself any favors–you won't gain many additional clients–solely by charging rates lower than the area standards.

Clients, particularly those more experienced and sophisticated, seldom fret over an agency's hourly rates. They are more concerned with the results that can be produced within their budget. If a client is worried about hourly rates, he or she can always find someone–such as a free-lancer–who is willing to work for less money. Don't sell yourself cheap. Charge competitive rates, but don't be afraid to raise them. Clients raise prices on their products for a multitude of reasons, and most clients do not expect you to operate as a nonprofit organization. Bear this in mind. A $5.00 per hour increase in your rates can mean at least an additional $6,000 income annually per person!

CONTROL COSTS

It's this simple; the best way to control costs is to avoid mistakes, whether by management or staff. Committing your firm to too much or too expensive space, costly furnishings or excessive salaries are management mistakes that can be avoided with a little forethought. (Most firms use a salary to income ratio of 50 percent as a goal and try to hold rent costs between 7 and 12 percent of income.)

Constantly and carefully examine and justify every overhead item. Arrange for the best possible deal on insurance and other employee benefits. Watch travel and entertainment expenses. Charge all possible costs back to your clients.

Train and motivate employees to avoid human mistakes that cost you money. Reprinting a client brochure or redistributing a press release because of a typo or incorrect information takes a chunk out of your bottom line (and doesn't do a whole lot for client relations or your agency's professional reputation).

USE YOUR TIME EFFICIENTLY AND PRODUCTIVELY

Sooner or later, to control and assure firm growth and profitability, most firm principals need to spend less time on client service and more time on firm management.

The closer you are to reaching or topping $1,000,000 in annual income, the more attention you should pay to managing your business. (A firm owner with profit problems once told me that she "hated to waste time looking at time sheets." Once she did–and corrected the problems she uncovered–her profit problem was also corrected.)

Carving out time for management tasks provides the flexibility and latitude to monitor and manage critical profit factors as well as develop and lead a proactive marketing program. Schedule regular and uninterrupted time to address problems and opportunities. Try not to spend more than half your time on client service; use the rest to manage and market your firm.

Follow these ten management strategies religiously and relentlessly and provide the best possible service to your clients, and your growth and profitability will be assured. Without attention to good management principles and practices, your firm's future will be dimmer than you would like, even with excellent client service. It's your choice!

PROFILE 10

CAROLE KERBEL, PRESIDENT, KERBEL COMMUNICATIONS INC., TORONTO

In 1974, Carole Kerbel was a mother with three small children doing free-lance publicity for nonprofit organizations. Today, she is president of a $3.2 million healthcare firm recognized as one of the most innovative in Canada.

Along the way, Kerbel managed a major switch in market niche from real estate clients to the multinational corporations and government bodies her 25-person firm serves today. From primarily promoting pharmaceutical products, her firm has expanded to offer such services as government relations, stakeholder relations, continuing health education, patient awareness and marketing counsel for such clients as Miles Canada, Merck Frosst, Bristol-Myers Squibb, and the Ministry of Health/Metro Toronto District Health Council.

Along the way, she also learned to: "Create a special niche for your firm and stick to it. However, take advantage of all the communication opportunities within that niche. (See above.) Promote your firm's successes, not yourself, through constant marketing."

Kerbel recommends that new principals ". . . do a lot of research (to find a market need) so that you don't create another 'me too' firm. Surround yourself with brilliant people and don't be afraid to pay to acquire top people. Make sure that you can handle the highs and lows of risk taking that come with being an entrepreneur."

Chapter 10

Managing Time and People

As the principal of a successful public relations firm, you should, at all times, be able to answer two basic and critical questions:

1. What are your three most serious problems; how are you dealing with them?
2. What are your three best opportunities; how will you take advantage of them? (Or is that four questions?)

Unfortunately, you may be so involved–so dedicated–to serving the daily needs of your clients, scratching out whatever business that falls in the door and performing routine duties, such as paying bills and meeting a payroll, that you fail to take time to think thoughtfully about long-range problems and opportunities, or to establish priorities for solving your problems and taking advantage of your opportunities.

Establishing and adhering to priorities requires that you manage your time–and that of your staff members–aggressively and productively.

The more efficiently and aggressively you manage your personal time, the more valuable you will be, both to your clients and your agency. To help you become more efficient and effective, keep a running list of your three most serious problems and your three best opportunities, either as they relate to your clients or your agency. Keep this list flexible and current.

PRIORITIZE PROBLEMS AND OPPORTUNITIES

Assign priorities to your problems. Here are three suggested priority categories:

1. Pressing–Solve it now, this instant, or face disaster.
2. Probable–It's a problem, but you have a jury rig fix on it and it probably won't explode immediately.
3. Potential–You can see this one coming but you have a little time to get ready for it.

How do your current problems fit these priorities?

Do the same with your opportunities. Here are three ways to prioritize opportunities:

1. Immediate–If you don't jump on it now, it will disappear forever.
2. Real–It's there, but you have a little time to decide how to approach it.
3. Potential–This one may or may not exist unless you make it happen.

Okay; ready, get set, go! Move on that fat opportunity.

DO IT NOW

To manage your time more aggressively, start with a "do it now" attitude. Attack even the most difficult or disagreeable tasks quickly. As the man said, "If you have to swallow a frog, don't look at it too long." Don't let distasteful tasks linger; get them out of the way quickly. Live with a daily "to do" list tied to your priority problems and opportunities. Decide what has to be done, when, and list priorities. Focus on the 20 percent of your effort that reaps 80 percent of the results. Teach and delegate routine work instead of feeling comfortable doing it.

Revise your lists daily; change priorities as required. Analyze "to do" lists against priorities. Take 15 minutes each day to plan the next day. Continually ask, "What is the best use of my time . . . now?"

DEAL WITH PAPER

Computers were supposed to create paperless offices and make waste baskets redundant. No way! Despite all the electronic marvels, paper continues to accumulate. And there are still only three things you can do with a piece of paper: pitch it, file it or act on it (even if you only send it to someone else). Number three is preferable.

Lots of people love paper. Piles of it on their desk give them a feeling of security. Rotund Royal Plenty was the former *Philadelphia Bulletin* business editor and a crackerjack investor relations pro in my Philadelphia PR firm. But the piles of paper on his desk left room only for an 8 1/2 × 11″ sheet of paper on which he scratched edits. Royal claimed he couldn't get used to not being able to sweep his desktop clean to the floor every night as he had at the *Bulletin* after writing his daily newspaper column. So he just left it there, but could find everything he needed. In his honor and to shame other careless souls, we created the "Royal Plenty Trash Award" and hung the engraved plaque outside erring practitioner's sloppy offices until they got the message.

The message is, make short work of paperwork. Here are some suggestions that you may have heard before:

- Pick up each piece of paper only once; try to do what has to be done with it the first time.
- Avoid new memos; write informal replies on the same sheet of paper.
- Don't let paper clutter your desk; throw away all the paper you can; file what you must keep; a good memory saves file retrieval time.

USE TIME WELL

It's an old cliche that once time has passed, you can never get it back; it's gone. The way you use your time will have a big impact on the success of your agency. Here are some suggestions:

- Avoid interruptions and delays; answer your own phone and make your own calls (unless you're under a deadline).
- Set ground rules with your receptionist about handling calls and unscheduled visitors when you're busy or in a meeting.
- Be punctual; expect others to be.

- Put dead time to use; do something productive when you're traveling in a plane, waiting in a lobby or otherwise twiddling your thumbs.
- Get in the "inside-lunch" habit.
- Make the most of meetings; set agendas; distribute them in advance; make sure every meeting generates action to solve problems; if there's nothing for an agenda, cancel the meeting.

And finally, stop believing in the virtue of "busyness" for its own sake. Don't mistake activity for accomplishment. Don't credit the most harried individual–even if that's you–with being the hardest working. Vow to work smarter instead of just harder.

MANAGING STAFF PRODUCTIVITY

A PR firm's primary source of income is the time its employees invest on behalf of clients at varying hourly rates. Ensuring that employees maintain the highest possible level of billable time (high productivity) is one of your most important responsibilities. High productivity hinges on pleasant working conditions, good employee morale and strong staff self-motivation. Both junior and senior practitioners should be empowered with the responsibility and authority to do whatever is necessary to meet performance standards and achieve client and firm goals.

ALLOCATING STAFF RESOURCES

Allocating the human resources of your firm properly–deciding who is going to do what and when–is an essential aspect of good agency management. Whether you do it for one, several or all your clients, you must plan, assign and balance work loads so that you can balance income flow and avoid problems caused by the cyclical nature of the agency business. Proper allocation of work loads also helps keep average staff productivity high and provides guidelines for determining short- and long-term staff needs. Here are some things to remember when you are allocating staff resources:

1. Everything works on averages over a period of time.
2. Allocation of staff time should be based on the average income generated by individuals or the average billable hour potential.
3. Determine overall and individual staff productivity averages. Taking into account average individual productivity and average hourly rates, determine the amount of income that the average practitioner can be expected to generate in a year. Multiply this figure by your total number of professional staff members. This represents the total time that can be assigned to clients and the total income that can be generated at your current staff level.
4. Example: At an average $85 per hour and 85 percent productivity, the average individual can be expected to generate about $100,000 per year in total time income. (The actual national average income generated annually per practitioner is about $130,000.)

Here is how the formula works: (NOTE: The figures are conservative and rounded off.)

1,400	Average number of hours an individual is actually available to work in 12 months–based on seven hours per day. Subtract vacations, holidays, sick days, and other time off from the 2,080 total number of hours in a year.
1,200	Average number of hours, an individual can be expected to bill to clients at 85 percent.
$100,000	1,200 hours times average hourly rate of $85 (actually $102,000).

Figure 10.1 (page 123) shows the staff allocation matrix that I used for about 15 years. (Figure 10.2, page 124, shows application of the matrix to a single client.) I thought that I had invented it until I discovered that other firms used the same system. The matrix can be used in both short- and long-range planning for both multiple and single clients and projects. It also takes into account staff capabilities, available staff time and specific client needs and budget.

The matrix can be designed and applied in pencil (so that it can be changed easily and frequently) or built into a computerized "what-if" template. Here's how the matrix works:

1. The ingredients
   a. List all your clients by three-letter initials down the left-hand column.
   b. List your professional staff members by initials across the top.
   c. List client budgets down the far right column.

2. The process
   a. Determine the amount of time required or available from assigned individuals for each account (convert hours to dollars).
   b. Assign dollars (or hours) per individual to meet individual client needs.
   c. Note both continuing needs and special short-term projects.
   d. In the second from the right column, add the total time allocated to each client against the budget.
   e. Add the assigned time for each individual at the bottom of each column.
   f. Determine shortfalls, overages and problems.
   g. Update the matrix weekly, monthly and annually.

Look ahead–on a structured basis–at both broad needs and individual client activity periods. Making adjustments in staff assignments on a weekly, monthly, quarterly and annual basis lets you spot and handle problems before they occur, and helps ensure smooth agency operations and satisfied clients.

DELEGATING RESPONSIBILITY AND AUTHORITY

One of the hardest things for many agency principals to learn or accept is delegation. They like to keep their hands on the wheel at all times. However, to be the most efficient and effective, you will need to delegate both responsibility and authority; responsibility to do the job and authority to get it done.

FIGURE 10.1. Resource Allocation Matrix (Multiple Clients)

Note: Average practitioner billable time = $100,000 over 12 months; $25,000 over 3 months −(Add three zeros below)

	Mgr	Helen	Ralph	Shirley	Paul	Time Shortage	Time Allocated	Annual Income
Client SMI	5	40			15		60,000	60,000
ABC	15		40	20	15	10	90,000	100,000
JON		10			30		40,000	40,000
WID				25			25,000	25,000
XYZ			10		20	10	30,000	40,000
COM			20*		10*		30,000	30,000
HOS	10	30		10			50,000	50,000
PIC	5	20		15			40,000	40,000
PEN				15		20	15,000	35,000
INK	10			15		15	25,000	40,000
DRI	10					30	10,000	40,000
PRO		(Pro bono - not billable)			10		(10,000)	0
NBD	45	10	(New business - not billable)				(55,000)	0
TOT	100	110	70	100	100	85	415,000	500,000

Problems:
1. Helen is overbooked (over $100,000).
2. Ralph is light; he's too specialized or too junior.
3. Shirley is split among too many accounts.
4. *Special project for client COM will require intense activity from two people over a two-month period. They will not be available to work on other accounts.
5. You will be almost one person short to meet all client needs and earn all the income budgeted over this 12-month period.

Solutions:
1. Look at the timetable of scheduled activities to determine if or when an additional person will need to be hired. Begin recruiting and interviewing.
2. Shift some of Shirley's accounts to Ralph. If Ralph can't handle the accounts, consider training or replacing him. You may need to upgrade this position with a more experienced person, able to handle a broader variety of business.
3. Shift pro bono work to a less skilled person with a lighter load (Ralph); Paul could then pick up some of Helen's assignments.
4. Don't accept project business unless you have enough staff flexibility to handle it.
5. Line up free-lancers to handle projects or heavy loads.

FIGURE 10.2. Resource Allocation Matrix (Individual Client - ABC)
Assign Individual's Time by Budgeted Activities
(Dollars allocated–Add three zeros)

Activity	Mgr	Ralph	Shirley	Paul	Shortage	Time Allocated	Income
Planning	5	2				7,000	7,000
Supv	5		10			15,000	15,000
New Prod		20				20,000	20,000
Features				10		10,000	10,000
Releases				5		5,000	5,000
Press Conference	3	10				13,000	13,000
Media Tour		4				4,000	4,000
VNR		4				4,000	4,000
Brochure					10*	0	10,000
Media Relations	2		10			12,000	12,000
TOTAL	15	40	20	15	10	90,000	100,000

Problems

1. * No one has time to produce the brochure.
2. * Paul is scheduled for some heavy writing chores at the same time that he's locked into the special project for client COM (see multiple-client matrix).

Solutions

1. Take Paul off the pro bono work to free time for him to handle a large part of the brochure.
2. Bring in free-lancers to handle other writing assignments.

The need to delegate applies to account executives as well as senior management. Letting someone else do it, when you think you could do it better, can be a bitter chore.

You can find lots of reasons why "I have to do it myself:"

1. I have to make sure it gets done right.
2. The client wants me to do it.
3. No one else has the time.
4. I have to do it so we won't go over budget.
5. I can do it better than anyone else.
6. It's faster to do it myself than to show someone.
7. I need something to do to look busy.
8. I don't want anyone else to know how to do it.
9. I don't want anyone else to know agency secrets.
10. I don't get to have any fun.
11. I like to do it.

If you've found yourself using any of the above reasons (even subconsciously) to avoid delegating a task or responsibility, catch yourself by the back of the neck and give yourself a good shake.

Why Delegate?

Delegating responsibility and authority to other people frees your time for things that only you can do or, at least, do better than others. Remember the rule that says you make the most profit when the most highly competent least costly people do most of the work.

In addition, and more important, people need increased independence and increased responsibility in order to grow. They grow by being taught, tested and critiqued and by observing, experimenting and doing. By delegating responsibility and authority to others, you will set a pattern for your senior people to follow and for others to copy.

How to Delegate

Let's be clear about it; delegation does not mean lowering your quality standards. Repeat: delegation does not mean lowering your quality standards! Follow these steps to ensure that quality is maintained while people are encouraged to stretch their minds and professional muscle.

1. Review the client's needs. What level of skill will be required to complete the task?
2. Evaluate the practitioner's ability and determine the amount and level of supervision required.
3. Set standards for the assignment; outline the results required.
4. Inform and instruct the practitioner; establish a realistic time-table for completion of the project.
5. Be flexible on the method and approach to be used. There are many ways to do things; not all of them the same as you would use, and that's not all bad.
6. Evaluate the effort. Be positive. Discuss changes. Offer suggestions and guidance. Do not redo the job yourself (unless you are absolutely out of time and budget).
7. Protect the agency; provide a protective but inconspicuous oversight. Let the junior person function on his or her own as much and as long as possible. Monitor; be aware of progress toward deadline. Don't threaten or pressure.
8. Be willing to risk; up to the point where you decide that you must step in immediately to avoid disaster. I can't tell you what that point will be. However, you'll know when you hit it. Go just a bit beyond your first warning before you step in or yank the assignment away.

PROFILE 11

ANNE KLEIN, PRESIDENT, ANNE KLEIN & ASSOCIATES, MT. LAUREL, NJ

Klein left the Sun Company in 1982 after 16 years of corporate, nonprofit and agency PR experience; the shrinking oil industry made her job security appear tenuous. However, she left with a one-year contract from Sun for her new PR agency. Operating from offices in the basement of her home, the firm's first year income hit $43,000; it has grown to ten employees and $1 million in revenue.

Lessons learned during those early years, according to Klein: "The owner of a firm cannot do everything or be involved in everything; working from home can only last so long if you want to grow; and managing the finances and growing the business are as important as delivering excellent service.

"We live by the rule 'good enough is not good enough.' But I learned that clients would not pay for the ultimate.

"I also learned that no one can build your business for you. You can listen and learn, hire consultants, but in the end, you build your business in the image you have for yourself. Before you start your firm, be sure you like to sell and that you have a good professional reputation.

"Love your existing clients; be visible; court your colleagues and potential clients. Schedule more time off of short duration rather than one long vacation; you can never look tired."

Chapter 11

Systems and Procedures

Flying an airplane by the seat of the pilot's pants went out of favor with the advent of aircraft that could fly faster than pilots could think. PR firm principals face much the same type of problem. Things move too fast in the agency business for you to guess where you've been and where you're going. While you are still trying to figure out whether you made any money last month, the waters of disaster may be lapping at your nose.

To keep your firm on the right track, you need administrative systems and procedures that generate business progress data, assure tight cost controls, track profitability and productivity and help you report promptly and properly to clients. Such systems can range from on-line computerized daily time reports to a method of establishing hourly billing rates that return a specific profit to a method of evaluating your firm's overall performance. Unfortunately, principals with great entrepreneurial instincts and professional strengths may lack the self-discipline to see the value of or adhere to such administrative parameters. Big mistake!

CLIENT AGREEMENTS

In addition to trust, confidence and chemistry, the foundation of every client-agency relationship should be a signed agreement stipulating the beginning date of the relationship, the terms of the agreement, the services to be performed, the financial arrangements agreed upon, a "hold harmless" clause and the conditions under which the agreement will be extended or terminated.

There may be occasions when the signing of such an agreement is delayed while the client's legal counsel earns his or her pay. However, you tempt fate by investing any substantial time or money on the new client's behalf until all signatures have been applied.

I learned this lesson painfully when my agency began working for a state-mandated but farmer-funded organization while the client's legal counsel "studied" the contract we had proposed. Weeks went by with no signed contract. "You know how lawyers are," the client explained several times. By then, we had invested thousands of dollars worth of time on the client's behalf.

Then, we were called into a meeting with the organization's executive director. Barricaded behind his desk, the client solemnly advised us that state law forbids any work to be done for his organization by outside agencies before a contract was signed. With a straight face, he said that since we had no contract, he obviously had never assigned us to do any work. This, despite an inch-thick file of conference reports. (We learned later that the executive director was madly back-pedaling to forestall being fired for violating state regulations.)

However, he said, his attorney would be happy to negotiate an agreement with our attorney. Stunned, and sitting on $75,000 worth of unpaid invoices, we submitted to the negotiation charade. *Three months later,* we signed a ten-page agreement! The next day we received a letter terminating our services. (We envisioned the client breathing a sigh of relief at his close call with a pink slip.) We ended up collecting about half of the amount due.

Moral Number 1: Never begin work for a client who hesitates to sign an agreement immediately. Moral Number 2: Never be a client's first PR agency, if you can avoid it. The hassle can drive you bonkers.

You should consult your attorney in the preparation of an agency-client agreement format that follows your state laws. Here is a sample letter of agreement that you may want to adapt for your use.

SAMPLE AGENCY-CLIENT AGREEMENT

DATE
NAME, TITLE, COMPANY/ORGANIZATION, ADDRESS
Dear _____ :

This letter, when signed by both parties, will constitute the agreement between us with regard to our representation as your public relations agency.

1. We agree to serve as your public relations agency in connection with the implementation of a public relations program on your behalf.
   a. As your agency, we will provide you with counsel on the public relations aspects of your policies, programs, and goals. In addition, we will perform other public relations and marketing-related activities.
2. For our services and outlays on your behalf, the basis of our compensation shall be as follows:
   a. For all counseling, planning, writing and placement services, we shall be entitled to:
      - A minimum advance fee of $ _____ per _____ for staff time charges.
      - Charges for services of our staff members will be made at then-standard hourly rates for officers and staff as they are required to carry out the programs and activities approved by you. Staff time charges incurred in any month will be applied against the minimum fee. Any staff time charges incurred above the minimum will be billed at then-existing standard rates.
   b. On all artwork and mechanical items purchased by us for you on your authorization, including printing, typesetting, photography, artwork and specialty items, you agree to pay us our cost plus the standard commission of 17.65 percent.
   c. You will reimburse us at cost for such outlays made by us on your behalf as travel, telephone, telegram, facsimile transmission, messenger, copies, freight, postage, taxes and similar expenditures. At our option, we may require advance payment by you for large out-of-pocket expenditures. You agree to pay same promptly upon request from us.
3. The following billing and due dates shall be in effect unless otherwise specified and agreed upon between us:
   a. The monthly fee will be due and payable within ten (10) days from date of receipt of invoice.
   b. Travel costs, messenger, postage and other similar expenditures (see 2c above) will be invoiced as incurred. All

invoices are payable within ten (10) days of receipt of invoice.

c. Payment for production invoices is due ten (10) days from receipt of invoice.

d. On invoices for which payment is not received within 30 days, you agree to pay us simple interest computed at Citibank Prime plus 1 1/2 percent per annum on the amount outstanding after 30 days of the invoice date until such payment is received.

e. In the event that you question the validity of a charge by us, payment for only that portion under question may be delayed without penalty, provided you express your objection in writing within twenty (20) days of the date of the invoice.

f. At our option, we may suspend work on your account should any invoice remain unpaid beyond sixty (60) days from date of said invoice.

4. We agree that any and all contracts, correspondence, books, accounts, and other sources of information relating to your business shall be available for inspection at our office by your authorized representative during ordinary business hours upon reasonable prior notice by you to us of your desire to inspect same.

5. Following in-person or telephone conferences between your representative and ours in which decisions are made concerning actions or work to be performed, we will submit a conference report summarizing decisions made. Unless you object in writing to the conference report within six (6) business days, that report will be considered an accurate summary of the conference.

6. The terms of this agreement shall commence on _____ and will continue unless and until terminated by either party on not less than ninety (90) days prior written notice to the other, delivered by registered or certified mail. The rights, duties and responsibilities of the parties hereto shall continue in full force until the expiration of the term.

7. Upon the expiration of this agreement, no rights or liabilities shall arise out of this relationship, except that any uncancel-

lable contracts made on your authorization and still existing at the expiration of the term shall be carried to completion by us and paid for by you in accordance with the provisions herein, unless mutually agreed in writing to the contrary.

8. Upon the termination of this contract and receipt of final payments, we shall transfer, assign and make available to you or your representative all property and materials in our possession or control which belong to you.

9. We agree to indemnify you with respect to any claims or actions for libel, slander, defamation, copyright infringement, idea misappropriation or invasion of rights of privacy arising out of any materials which have been prepared by us on your behalf, except that if any such claim or action is based upon materials supplied by you to us, then, in such event, the aforesaid shall not apply, and in turn, you will indemnify and hold us harmless with respect thereto. In addition, we agree to indemnify you with respect to any other claims or actions based upon the contents of any publicity material prepared by us without your approval, and you agree to indemnify us with respect to any such claims or actions based upon the content of any such materials which have been supplied by you to us.

10. We covenant and agree that we:

   a. Shall keep confidential any and all information concerning your business and operation which becomes known to us by reason of the performance of our services as your public relations agency and which information you advise us in writing that you consider to be confidential in nature.

   b. Shall not disclose any such confidential information to any person outside our employ unless to do so is required in connection with the performance of our services and in such event, we agree to utilize our best efforts to obtain from any such suppliers a similar agreement to maintain such information as confidential.

   c. Shall obtain from our employees who in the performance of services on your behalf may become privy to any such confidential information, a similar covenant and agreement to keep confidential all such information.

11. You agree not to hire or retain directly or indirectly any person employed full time by this agency during the terms of this Agreement or for one year after termination of this Agreement unless we approve in writing or you pay the equivalent of twice the employee's annual salary at time of separation from this agency. "Indirectly" includes you hiring or contracting with another firm which employs an individual employed by us.

If the above meets with your approval, kindly indicate your consent by signing where indicated below.

Very truly yours,

AGENCY NAME

By _____

Title_____

ACCEPTED AND AGREED:

By _____

Title _____

Date _____

Some clients may object to signing individual paragraphs, such as the interest penalty clause, of an agreement like the above. Depending on how strongly you feel about such clauses, you may want to question whether you should establish a relationship with a client who nitpicks an agreement. And when your new client says he has not signed the agreement because, "Our attorney still has it," believe that about as much as the one about the check being in the mail.

ESTABLISHING CLIENT-AGENCY EXPECTATIONS

There are few more teeth-grinding, nerve-fraying, sanity-sapping experiences than trying to work efficiently, effectively and profitably for a client who has no public relations experience.

Mental trauma also can occur when you are the client's first agency. In such cases, the words "realistic" and "expectations" seldom appear in context or in client-agency discussions.

Another threat to agency principals' mental balance is the client executive who, although several layers removed from his or her company's day-to-day PR activities, wields control over PR programs, budgets and invoice approval. And who can wipe out a recommended program with an infuriating shake of his head or drive you silly by nitpicking invoices to bits.

It may also be true, as some bitter souls contend, that clients begin to hate (and/or fear) their agency immediately upon hiring them. Your client contact may have had a bad experience with a previous agency and is anticipating a similar disappointment. He may not have been comfortable with his role in the agency selection process or may doubt his ability to move the agency swiftly and productively into the traces.

The PR executive may have promised senior executives that the agency could and would produce great wonders. Everyone may be waiting eagerly for your first big media hit. They also may be holding their breath in anticipation of your first big bill. And you are still celebrating the win!

If you should become transfixed by one or more of these unhappy circumstances, you are likely on the way to becoming an endangered species. The truth is that too-great, often-unrealistic expectations are the norm and too frequently the cause of serious client-agency fallout.

One of the best ways to prevent or diminish such friction is to teach the client what he or she can realistically expect from the agency and what the agency expects from its clients. Do it early on, before the relationship has time to sour. As Tom Gable, president of The Gable Group, San Diego, CA puts it in his firm's Client Service Manual:

"Since agencies toil in the field of communication, they should be clever enough to tactfully share with clients some instructions that reflect the client's part in building strong unions. While this sharing won't necessarily be accomplished in a single document or afternoon, the points should be made. For instance, an agency can suggest that its clients:

- Adjust expectations to reality and rely on the agency for 'reality checks' as to where the company is headed vis à vis the market and its competition.

- Be a partner with the agency; work together for mutual success.
- Allow the agency to make a fair profit on the business.
- Avoid seeking something for nothing. Expect to pay for program development and creative thought.
- Set clear business objectives upon which the agency can build its program in the company's behalf; a client should not expect the agency to write its marketing and business plan (unless hired and paid for that purpose).
- Be responsive and available, both for approvals and media contact.
- Respect the professionalism of agency staff and match it internally.
- Appreciate that the agency will never know as much about your business as you do; nor should it be expected to. Benefit from its independent point of view and ability to translate the essence of your business for multiple audiences.
- Pay bills promptly. If there is a question or concern, deal with it right away.
- If not a public relations executive, learn the basics of the profession."

Reprinted with permission of Tom Gable, President, The Gable Group.

RELATIONSHIP COVENANT

You also may want to insert a "Relationship Covenant" on your standard letter of agreement. The Covenant could read:

We understand that you expect the agency to invest a consistently high level of skill, creativity and professional performance on your behalf so as to generate a substantial return on your investment and advance your business objectives. We also understand that you expect to receive timely, honest and descriptive invoices that are supported by meaningful backup information. We are committed to the fulfillment of these expectations.

In return, we will expect high levels of understanding, support, patience and professionalism as well as realistic performance requirements from you. We expect to be paid promptly.

The realization of these mutual expectations will provide the core and sustenance of a mutually satisfying and long-lasting relationship between our organizations.

Clients are seldom reluctant to outline their expectations (if they know them) or to complain when they are not met. It therefore seems appropriate and realistic that agencies follow suit. Performance and commitment on both sides are keys to good client-agency relationships. But the client may never know what you expect in terms of his performance and commitment . . . unless you tell him.

TECHNOLOGY IN PR FIRM MANAGEMENT

(I am indebted for the following section on the use of technology by PR firms to William Boehlke, managing officer, Phase Two Strategies, a San Francisco high tech firm. When in doubt, ask an expert. Says Bill:)

"Surveys of clients indicate that the perception of low value for the money is the greatest marketing problem faced by our industry. In response, PR firms must identify ways to achieve more results for the same budgets. We have found that an ongoing investment of roughly 10 percent of fee income in technology (for capital equipment, supplies, and labor) helps us improve client service, maintain profit margins and give clients about 6 percent more results for the money each year. We also have found that we get a substantial reduction in overhead costs that offsets our technology expenditure even before considering the benefits to client service.

"Automating a PR firm starts with the personal computer. Think of your personal computers as tools that deliver services to the user that help him practice more effectively. Professionals will usually be working on several active tasks so the monitor screen should be big; a minimum 17 inches. A large display and graphical operating system, such as Microsoft Windows or the Macintosh, means people can easily work with the different software applications and projects they will need during a typical day.

"As you acquire computers, consider buying laptops with docking stations. For a small premium, your staff gets a machine they can take with them when they leave the office. Remote access software will let them connect to the office wherever they may be and be just as productive as they would be at their desk. When they're not on the road, the docking station gives them a full-sized keyboard, display and a network connection.

"A network is the single most important prerequisite for a substantial return on your investment in technology. Public relations is collaborative; a single copy of all shared information must be immediately accessible to the professionals who need it.

"Shared information should be delivered through one or more centralized data bases. In the early days of public relations, practitioners considered the Rolodex a strategic asset. Today, the data base does the same job, better. Every practitioner in the firm can have access to the complete history of all the firm's contacts with an editor or analyst.

"The other important network application is electronic mail, to replace paper memos. E-mail saves time internally, but more important benefits come from links to client E-mail systems and to the many editors who prefer receiving pitch letters and releases electronically.

"Your telephone should be as integrated with your computers as you can afford. Software can look up numbers and dial phone calls. Other software can send facsimiles without walking to the fax machine. Cellular phones can be integrated into most modern phone systems, so clients can reach you wherever you are. And as digital telephone service becomes widely available, there will come a time when the phone rings and a record of your past conversations and meetings with the caller appears on your screen before you pick up the handset.

"Research is another area where technology has a big impact. For many practitioners, online research has been difficult and expensive to use. Today, shared CD-ROM data bases can provide everyone in your firm with fast access to information such as recent business coverage in metro newspapers. Electronic links to wire services mean you can act on information about your client's competitors the minute it is announced and store it so you can search it in the future without the cost of going on-line. When information is free and easy to access, it gets used for activities ranging from coverage reviews to competitive analysis.

"Your computers also can help you manage your business better. Job cost software, with which practitioners complete time entries as they work throughout the day, makes invoice preparation fast and easy, and can produce activity reports and profitability analyses with little additional effort. Software can give you daily information about what your employees worked on and billed to your clients. More importantly, it gives managers a quick way to make detailed work assignments to staff members. It also helps keep everyone on track to produce the results you told your clients to expect.

"Information technology will continue to help agencies deliver more results for the same client budget dollar every year. Firm principals who plan to grow beyond a few clients should have a plan for managing this area of their business."

Reprinted with permission of William Boehlke, Managing Officer, Phase Two Strategies.

COST ACCOUNTING
("THE GOSPEL ACCORDING TO HARRY")

A few years ago, when I was learning to manage a profitable public relations firm, the guru of "Cost Accounting and Budgetary Control" was Harry A. Cooper, Vice President, Finance, Hill & Knowlton. Cooper wrote a monograph published by the Public Relations Society of America's Counselors Academy that outlined the basic systems and procedures needed by a well-managed public relations firm.

Some 30 years later, the "Gospel According to Harry" is still being sung by the choir (without many of the choir members knowing where the words and music came from). Cooper's dictums are applied by many PR firms; perhaps by most well-managed firms. If you are a member of the Counselors Academy, I recommend that you get a copy of his monograph which is still in print. If you are not a member, it's worth joining just to get your hands on Cooper's masterpiece.

Following Cooper's guidelines, your accounting and budget control systems should generate:

1. The basis for accurately billing your clients for the services you provide.
2. A monthly tabulation of your firm's operating income and expenses. Expenses will be of two types: (A) Cost to the firm; or (B) Outside purchases that will be rebilled to clients.
3. The means to determine whether your payroll costs are chargeable (to clients) or nonchargeable (having to do with time off or administrative, new business or agency chores).
4. Monthly reports of both overall profitability (or loss) and individual client profitability.

There are four things that you will need to know regularly and accurately: the number of dollars that the firm generates through hourly time billing and markup of outside purchases; the amount of overall profit that the firm earns (both pre- and post-taxes); the amount of profit earned on each client; and the level of productivity (billable hours) for the firm and individual staff members.

TIME REPORTS

Since the days when B.C. Neanderthal and Associates hunter-gatherers chiseled a record of their billable hours on stone tablets, public relations agency practitioners and support staff have historically fought—and often neglected—the necessity to account for their daily time in small increments, usually in 15-minute blocks. Frequently, the agency principal and other senior executives are the most guilty of this infraction. (Some years ago, a Ketchum PR account executive temporarily overcame her distaste for the task by compiling her time sheets a week in advance—until I caught on to her sudden promptness.)

The fact is that almost everything that is basic about the financial life of a PR firm rests on daily time reports filed by everyone from secretaries to the president.

Individuals' time reports can be submitted on traditional paper time sheets or via an on-line computer software program tied into your accounting software. As with many things, agencies seem to follow no particular pattern in their requirements for reporting staff time. While agencies may opt for daily, weekly or semi-monthly reports, I recommend that time be reported and put into your software program daily. At the very least, employees should maintain a daily record of the way they spend their time, if only through cryptic scrawling on a desk calendar.

As every agency employee quickly learns, it is difficult enough to remember, in some detail, what you were doing 24 hours earlier without trying to recall exactly what you did a week earlier.

Both time that is chargeable to a client and time that is not chargeable should be reported. Sometimes (sometimes too often), time will be invested on behalf of a client but not billed to that client. In such cases, the nonchargeable time becomes part of the cost of servicing the account. Therein lies the source of the dreaded "write-down" or "write-off" in which time, and related dollars, that should have been billed to a client are wiped from memory, lost forever in a sea of red ink. Nonchargeable time, of course, can also be expended in justifiable agency support activities such as publicity, promotion and new business solicitation.

Paper time sheets and on-line computer systems generally require individuals to record such data as: an employee number; client codes–usually three initials; a job number; the amount of time invested in specific projects; a brief description of the service provided or work completed; and a record of time off (vacation, holiday, illness) and other nonchargeable activities. Employees are required to account for a minimum number of hours each day depending on the normal working hours of the firm (7, 7 1/2 or 8 hours).

If an employee works more than the standard number of hours in a day, these additional hours should also be recorded. Weekend hours are recorded in the same way. Account people who need–or take–more time to complete a project than a client's budget permits may be tempted to put in the extra hours in the evening or on a weekend and not report the time so that the extra time does not become visible or billable. Not a good idea; in fact, a bad idea!

Such behavior reduces agency income and leads to an unrealistic picture of account profitability by indicating that fewer than the actual number of hours were required to complete the project. It also paints a false picture of the employee's productivity and prevents future budgets on similar projects from being adjusted upward.

Employees must be directed to report their time candidly and accurately without being concerned that their time sheets–perhaps indicating a number of unbillable or excessive hours–may reflect badly on their performance or on their job or financial security. Encourage employees to maintain high productivity and stick within client budgets. However, understand and accept that there will always be instances when, for understandable and acceptable reasons, the employe can do neither. A sudden budget cut, an incorrect budget estimate, a client decision delay, or any number of uncontrollable circumstances can leave a practitioner with a lot of unbillable time on his or her hands. In such cases, accurate time reports will give you reliable information on which to base management decisions. (See examples of paper and on-line time reports in Appendixes A and B.)

SETTING HOURLY RATES

Public relations agencies use different systems to establish hourly billing rates. Many agencies try to simplify the process by applying variations of an inaccurate but historically popular "X times direct salary cost" method combined with "what the market will bear."

Unfortunately, this simplistic approach does not take into account rising overhead expenses, in particular, today's high cost of technology and employee health care benefits.

As Harry Cooper said all those years ago: "Good financial planning demands that the overhead factor must be taken into consideration in the setting of any client billing rates . . . . It also demands that all items of overhead are controlled and maintained at the absolute minimum level." Well said, Harry! Especially in Cooper's time when many PR firm principals were taking the easy way out by using two and a half times direct salary as the base for hourly rates. Today, the formula is more likely three and a half or four times the salary costs. However, it's still wrong. Harry had it right then . . . and now.

Although more complex than the "X times salary cost" system (which actually is more of a guessing game than a management system), the most practical and profit-generating system that I know of–that I first read about in Harry Cooper's monograph–utilizes the following three factors as the base for hourly billing rates:

1. Annual salary costs (including benefits), plus;
2. Overhead percentage, plus;
3. Profit percentage desired.

This total is then divided by the expected number of annual billable hours per person to arrive at the hourly rate that is required to achieve the desired profit percentage.

An individual's annual salary costs include both his actual salary and an expression of benefit costs, either actual individual costs or a percentage share.

To determine your overhead percentage, divide your total overhead costs (including nonchargeable staff salaries; i.e., secretaries, receptionists, etc.) by your total direct salary costs. This overhead percentage figure–generally plus or minus 100 percent–is added to salary costs for an individual or a group of employees. (The more you reduce overhead costs and the overhead percentage, the higher your profits will be and the lower your hourly rates can be to reach the desired profit.)

To set hourly rates that will generate 25 percent profit, add a 33 1/3 percent profit factor to the sum of salary and overhead costs. To achieve 20 percent profit, add a 25 percent profit factor; for a 15 percent profit, add a 20 percent profit factor.

Divide this total by the number of expected annual billable hours to arrive at the appropriate hourly rate.

Here are two examples of the system at work:

Salary Cost	Overhead @ 80%	Sub-Total	Profit Factor @33 1/3%	Total	Annual Billable Hours	Hourly Rate
$ 50,000	$40,000	$ 90,000	$30,000*	$120,000	1,500	$80
$100,000	80,000	180,000	60,000*	240,000	1,200	$200

(*–Equals 25 percent of "Total")

For convenience, instead of establishing different rates for each individual, you can group employees by title or salary increments (e.g., every $5,000).

While the above is a commonly accepted system, firms use a number of other methods to set hourly rates. However, all of these alternate methods utilize the same basic data. The primary variation is in the number of hours that practitioners are expected to bill annually. (For some reason, PR agencies cannot agree on a standard for the average number of hours that a practitioner should reasonably be expected to bill annually.) Here are several examples of other systems:

- National Firm–Determines annual salary costs for a practitioner by adding a 4 percent salary increase factor and 22 1/2 percent for cost of benefits to actual salary. Divides by 1,540 hours to arrive at hourly rate.
- West Coast Firm–Multiplies salary by 128 percent for benefits and divides by 1,612 hours. Then adds a 70 percent overhead factor to arrive at the hourly salary cost. For most mid-range account people, who spend all their time serving clients, a 50 percent profit factor is added to reach the billing rate. Account coordinators and senior people who spend less time actually servicing clients are not billed at as high a profit factor. Here is how the system works:

$50,000.	Annual salary
14,000.	28 percent for benefits.
64,000.	Divided by 1,612 hours
40.	Cost per hour
28.	Plus overhead of 70 percent
68.	Total hourly cost
34.	Plus profit of 50 percent
100.	Hourly billing rate

- Midwest Firm–Divides direct salary costs by 2,080 hours and adds 20 percent for benefits. Uses these factors plus a 150 percent overhead factor to monitor client profitability. However, billing rates are pretty much set by what the market will bear.
- West Coast Firm–Uses four times direct salary costs to set hourly rates. Rates are set by job title.

Harry Cooper's system is still the best!

REPORTING TO CLIENTS

One of your most important responsibilities is to establish and maintain a good flow of information to and from your clients. Get in the habit of putting things in writing. Confirm client decisions and instructions. Keep your client contact informed of details of ongoing programs as well as of meetings and projects that he or she might not be involved in regularly.

A good two-way flow of information prevents misunderstandings and offers excellent CYA benefits. Sometimes, you might think that all this paperwork is too much bother–or that it is costing the client too much. (I've even seen the rare client who didn't want a lot of reports. Such clients were told that a full reporting system was an agency policy.)

However, I guarantee that the day will come when you will be grateful that you have a piece of paper confirming that the client gave you certain instructions or approved a specific project or cost . . . some time in the past. Long after you have both forgotten the details of the project.

Here is a good rule to follow: Any time a client provides information, gives you instructions, makes a decision or approves something . . . CONFIRM IT IN WRITING AND SEND THE CLIENT A COPY.

The Paper Flow

Here is a quick review of the "paper" (could be Fax or E-mail) that should flow from your firm to your clients. Copies of these reports should be distributed as broadly as possible within the client organization to not only ensure that senior executives understand the progress of the public relations program, but to merchandise the agency's accomplishments.

Conference Report

This report confirms the understandings reached, instructions given or approvals granted in every meeting, conference or contact between agency and client personnel whether live or by telephone.

It usually follows a standard format, often on "Conference Report" letterhead with space for the client's name and the meeting date and conference report date. The format may contain sections for "Activity," "Action to be taken," "Action timetable," and "Action responsibility."

Conference reports confirming client financial commitments are especially important. Reports should be completed and sent to the client as soon as possible, no later than 48 hours after the conference.

Be sure your clients understand that the agency will act in accordance with information contained in conference reports unless the client refutes the report contents within a reasonable time; two to five days. (See client agreement example.)

A former client was fond of scheduling weekly meetings with the full agency account team. Before the conference report covering each meeting was distributed, a draft version was sent to the client contact so that he could make sure that we had described the meeting the way he "remembered" it. Sometimes, after the client's "corrections," it seemed like we hadn't all attended the same meeting.

Monthly Quarterly Status Report

This report covers the progress and status of the agency's assignments over the past month or quarter. The report should accompany monthly invoices or follow shortly. It provides an opportunity for the client to evaluate agency charges against results and work in progress.

A thoroughly detailed status report can answer or defuse a client's questions about the invoice. It also helps increase the agency's visibility and appreciation within the client's organization and can help increase the client contact's stature within his or her company.

With the client contact's approval, the report should be distributed broadly within the client organization. This helps merchandise and increase respect for the agency's work.

The report also serves as a control mechanism for agency senior account managers by indicating the account team's progress for the client and the work that remains to be completed. It also ensures that senior agency executives–who may not be involved in all daily work for the client–can respond logically and calmly to a client complaint.

The first page of each status report should be a brief "Highlights" section made for quick reading by senior client executives.

Write tersely. Summarize significant accomplishments; sell the value of the program and the agency's activities. Provide enough detailed information to reflect the firm's total effort and results achieved.

Media Contact Report

This report informs clients of routine contacts with media and reminds them that you are working in their behalf even when they may not see very much happening. It also ensures that the client is not caught off guard if a reporter mentions a conversation with an agency representative when he calls the client, and it ensures that no media request is accidentally overlooked.

Prompt and detailed reporting of your activities in clients' behalf is essential in maintaining a positive professional relationship. A good flow of agency reports also helps merchandise agency accomplishments and emphasizes account stewardship.

AGENCY PERFORMANCE AUDIT

Here is a way to take a hard look at the overall performance of your firm. You can use the "Agency Performance Audit" to gauge how well you are serving your clients and managing your business.

Each performance area has an arbitrary ten-point value with a total of 160 points. Give your firm an objective and honest score in each area. A "ten" means you are doing everything you should and/or as well as you possibly could in that area. Total the points. And look at your firm in the mirror.

You might want to ask your staff members or senior people to rate your firm the same way. They won't be able to answer all the questions, however, their opinions could be revealing. Agencies also use the Performance Audit as the basis for discussion at staff meeting or retreats.

AGENCY PERFORMANCE AUDIT

	Perfect Score	Your Score
Creativity on behalf of clients	10	_____
Innovation on behalf of clients	10	_____
Strategic planning for clients	10	_____
Concern for clients' interests	10	_____
Success in producing client results	10	_____
Success in retaining clients	10	_____
Agency long-range planning	10	_____
Agency strategic positioning	10	_____
New business effectiveness	10	_____
Account management	10	_____
Agency financial management	10	_____
Agency personnel management	10	_____
Vendor relations	10	_____
Facilities and equipment	10	_____
Rate of profit/income growth	10	_____
Agency's general reputation	10	_____
PERFECT SCORE	**160**	_____

MIRROR, MIRROR ON THE WALL . . .

140 and above	Excellent
120 - 139	Pretty good
100 - 119	Fair
80 - 99	Woeful
60 - 79	Awful
Below 60	Get a new job!

After you look at your firm in the mirror, on a separate piece of paper, write down the action required to improve each area that scored lower than seven or eight. Indicate the person responsible for the action, if it isn't you. Follow up to make sure the action is taken. Six months from now, grade your firm again. Repeat the test every six to 12 months.

PROFILE 12

DONNA BROOKS LUCAS, PRESIDENT, BR&R COMMUNICATIONS, CHICAGO, IL

"We were part of Burson-Marsteller and though clients loved our creativity, they wanted a black-owned firm. So we decided to take it out," says Brooks Lucas.

Now one of the few minority-owned PR firms, BR&R Communications generated $368,000 in revenue during its first year (1990) from such big-name clients as Baxter Healthcare, Sara Lee Corporation, and S.C. Johnson Wax. Today, the firm has $1 million income, nine employees, 20 clients and continues to serve national consumer and health care clients.

"Very often, we become the bridge between (our clients) and the community. However, we also are accountable to the African-American and Hispanic communities (that we work with). We make sure that a corporation isn't just throwing money at a problem and doing something wrong for the community.

"On one side, we're accountable to the community. On the other, we're more than happy to use and leverage our relationships, our expertise and our trust on our clients' behalf."

Today, the integrated marketing communications firm works in such fields as health care, consumer marketing, community relations, corporate communications, design and graphics, special events and videotape productions.

Advice to firm principals: "Create a business plan and stick to it. If done well, it will be your road map for the next five years."

Chapter 12

Forecasting Income
and Managing Profitability

One of your most important tasks is to accurately forecast the amount of income that can be expected from clients during a given period of time; a month, a quarter, six months or a year. You will need this information to anticipate cash flow and profit–how much money you will take in and how much you will keep–and to plan staff schedules and anticipate hiring additional employees.

There are important distinctions between forecasting and budgeting. (See Chapter 13 for an in-depth discussion of client budgeting.) Forecasting projects the amount of income that your firm will generate in a given period of time, based on work that actually will and/or can be completed. Budgeting is more pragmatic. It outlines the maximum cost of client projects and the total income available to the firm. Accurate forecasting is an essential aspect of both short- and long-range business planning.

There are both similarities and differences between budgeting and forecasting. They are both based on your ability to estimate how much staff time will be required to complete specific client activities and, therefore, how much agency income can be expected in payment for that work. Large amounts of commission or markup on production projects should also be included in income forecasts.

Budgeting establishes the cost parameters within which you must work. To produce an accurate income forecast, you must predict precisely how much work you will actually do within a specific time period and within budget parameters. The budgeting process may cover a longer period of time than forecasting.

For example, the client may have approved a total budget of $50,000 to cover the introduction of a new product over a three-month period. Forecasting requires that you estimate how much income the agency will receive during each of those three months based on the pace and amount of work required each month. For example, $10,000 the first month, $15,000 the second and $25,000 the third. And that means being able to establish and maintain realistic staff work schedules.

Forecasting income requires knowing the amount of time that you and other staff members will have available to invest in specific client projects within a time period.

Forecasting income also requires an understanding of both the activity that can be completed within a given period–because the client has approved it and/or budgeted for it and staff time is available–as well as the activity that must be completed within that period because it is time sensitive.

Time-sensitive activities include projects such as a special event tied to an athletic contest, a new product introduction that must precede the advertising campaign or press material related to a specific holiday season or special publication issue.

Of course, variables such as unforeseen or last minute assignments, opportunities, crises, the client decision-making process and other client idiosyncrasies will always have an impact on how much and what type of work is performed and, therefore, will affect the amount of income that is actually earned in any given period.

FORECAST FACTORS

Here are some other factors that can impact on the accuracy of your income forecast:

1. Client manufacturing schedules–Will the product be ready in time?
2. Client legal/approval process–Will the legal department forbid or delay the release of the copy or require extensive rewrite?
3. Client marketing and advertising plans–When is the client's advertising campaign scheduled to break?
4. Time schedule/availability of client contact–Are the client's priorities the same as the agency's? Is your client busy with so many other responsibilities that agency projects are delayed?

5. The experience/status of your client contact–Is your client contact experienced enough or respected enough within his or her company to push your work through and get approvals?
6. Corporate financial status–Are the corporation's sales falling off to the extent that PR budgets may be stretched out or eliminated?

For the most part, you have no control over any of the above factors. On the other hand, you do have some control over the amount of agency staff time that can be harnessed within a time period to meet client needs.

You can juggle your staff time commitments to meet varying client priorities. If you expect to be up to your ear lobes in the logistics and promotion of a major special event for one client that must happen in a specific time period, you may have trouble completing work for other clients during that time unless you anticipate the problem and take steps to solve it.

Being able to accurately forecast activity and income for one client will help assure that required work can be completed for other clients. Anticipating client needs well in advance–by forecasting anticipated income–also may indicate that you will need to either change client schedules, if possible, change staff assignments or call on free-lancers to help you through the time bind. Spreading the work load around between staff members assures that not only are client needs fully met but that available income is actually earned as anticipated.

Despite all the gremlins and glitches that can affect income forecasts, try to make your crystal ball view as accurate and timely as possible, neither overly optimistic nor pessimistic. On the other hand, it is also a good idea to be conservative when forecasting income. It's much easier to deal with more income than was expected than the reverse.

If you have acquired the ability to develop realistic budgets, the chances are good that your income forecasts will also be realistic and vice versa.

MANAGING PROFITABILITY

In addition to reliable income forecasts, your firm's profitability depends on vigorous and consistent control of such profit drains as high salary to income ratio, high overhead and operating costs including rent (your second largest expense after salaries), low staff productivity and unbillable client time. Nonbillable expenses, such as agency promotion, new business development, travel and client entertainment must be budgeted and contained.

Establish and live within a realistic overall firm budget. Charge fair, competitive, and profitable hourly rates, and track the profitability of each client. Either turn around or resign unprofitable clients.

THE FIVE MOST POPULAR WAYS TO LOSE MONEY

The five most popular (i.e., most common) ways that public relations firms lose money (or reduce profits):

1. Low productivity;
2. Write-offs;
3. Unprofitable clients;
4. Human mistakes; and
5. Excessive salary costs.

Low Productivity

Billable averages below 85 percent of the time practitioners are available to work may be the leading contributor to less than desirable or possible income and profit.

Billable averages as low as 60 percent are not uncommon. Consider this: a single account executive billing only 60 percent of his or her time at $90 per hour can cost your firm more than $30,000 a year in lost income.

A Midwest firm principal admitted that his firm's low productivity over a two-year period, including a 62 percent billable average during the second year, had reduced the firm's income and led to flat earnings. Additional income was available from clients, but went unearned because employees had not hustled enough to generate the extra revenue.

An unfortunate side effect of this kind of problem, of course, is that when practitioners are not hustling–have little or no sense of urgency–the quality of client service often suffers. Fortunately, in the above case, the firm avoided client criticism.

The only acceptable excuse for low productivity is a lack of enough business to keep employees busy. That places the responsibility for low productivity primarily on the firm principal who is burdened with the need to both generate new business and ensure that current clients are well served.

The simple fact is that a PR firm will only be as successful as its employees are motivated to get off their duffs and produce. Employees must be trained to understand and be enthusiastic about the fact that they represent the agency's primary source of income. (As Joey Reiman, President, the Joey Reiman Agency, Atlanta, told a PRSA Counselors Academy conference, "If employees are not fired with enthusiasm, they will be fired with enthusiasm.") However you choose to motivate employees, with a hammer or honey, only you can provide the needed spark.

The Midwest firm with low productivity boosted productivity abruptly with a giant, guaranteed-amount, all-or-nothing, first quarter bonus carrot. Total income had to meet management's goal. Either everyone got a bonus or no one did. Not my favorite motivation method and likely to be difficult to maintain on a continuing basis. However, in this case, the jump start worked. The firm has never again paid an all-or-nothing bonus but continues to reward individual employees for extra performance.

Write-Offs

Referred to as "write-offs," "write-downs" or "cuts," the unhappy practice of not charging clients for all the staff time that has been invested on their behalf can cost your firm hundreds of thousands of dollars annually. (Are you wincing because I just struck a nerve?)

Here again, you must bear the onus for the problem. You must ensure that your staff maintains high client service quality but does not over-service clients unnecessarily and does not make dumb mistakes. Remember that most clients are not willing to pay for perfection. (Here is that dual responsibility to manage the potential conflict between your clients' need for service and your agency's need for profits!)

Establish and stick to realistic budgets. Insist that employees invest no more time on clients' behalf than can be billed. As discussed in Chapter 11, insist that employees do not do client work on their own time without charging it to clients. (Whether it actually gets billed to clients is a later decision.) Hire practitioners who are competent, have a sense of urgency, can adhere to budgets and have the confidence to stop work before they invest too much time.

Unprofitable Clients

Not all clients are profitable. (Or had you already discovered that?) If you're stuck with an unrealistic low fee, the client's work requires too much time from senior people or you consistently write off large amounts because of excessive client demands or a faulty budget estimate–and there is no way to turn the account around to make it profitable–consider resigning it.

If an account is unprofitable because you budgeted incorrectly in the first place, you may be stuck with it unless you have a very understanding and generous client. Perhaps you can plead temporary insanity, throw yourself on the client's mercy, explain your loss on the client's account, and gain additional funds. But don't count on it. (Some agencies have managed to write a guaranteed profit into a client agreement. But that can get messy and give clients too much control over your business. I have seen cases where agencies were required to get client approval before granting employee salary increases.)

If program parameters change, i.e., the client decides to take a different direction or otherwise changes the ball game, you must confront him with two alternatives: increase the budget or eliminate previously scheduled activity.

On the other hand, there may be good reason to keep an unprofitable client on the books, at least temporarily. The client's check may help pay your rent and electric bill. It may be a good name to have on your client list, or you may be able to do good work for the client that helps you get other business.

I once found it impossible to nudge a machine tool manufacturer's profitability much above 4 percent because of the amount of time required from two high-salaried people. However, it was a well-respected company and the work and results we produced for the client were converted to case histories that helped win other business. So the client stayed on the books.

The difference was that I knew exactly the amount of profit the client was returning, why the profit was low and whether anything could be done about it. With that information, I could make an informed decision about the company's future as an agency client.

Two other examples: A Los Angeles firm resigned a major food service operator's coop shortly after winning it because the client demanded the agency assign eight full-time people, in addition to the firm principal, to a $330,000 annual fee. A Washington, D.C. firm consistently handled large highly visible public events which were minimally, if at all, profitable. However, because of the events' high visibility and the good results produced, the firm was awarded other more profitable business.

Unfortunately, many principals don't know the profitability of individual clients and cannot make informed decisions. Available computer programs can take care of that.

Human Mistakes

Blunders that lead to eating out-of-pocket expenses can cost thousands of dollars. (I know. I remember $10,000 in out-of-pocket costs that we washed down the drain because a tiny technical typo snuck through both agency and client proofreading, not to be discovered until the brochure was printed. The client said it was our mistake, even though he had signed off on the brochure, because he had given us the correct data in writing. I had to agree with him, but it ruined my P&L statement for that month and most of the rest of the year.) Staff training and motivation, careful proofreading, proper vendor instructions and tight supervision are the answer.

Excessive Salary Costs

Your salary to income ratio should be no more than 50 to 55 percent (60 to 65 percent if you include payroll taxes in your salary calculations). Your ratio will soar higher than it should if you have too many employees, do not have the proper balance between junior and senior people, salaries (including yours) are higher than industry averages (or your cash flow can accommodate) or your hourly rates are too low.

The answer to all of these problems is proper planning, budgeting and management.

LIVE WITHIN A REALISTIC BUDGET

If you have not developed an annual budget for your firm, here is a realistic guideline to help you reach that magical 20 to 25 percent pre-tax profit level (see Figure 12.1). It's also a reminder of the types of expenses that you should anticipate and include in your firm's annual budget.

Base your budget on the amount of income (not your firm's total billing which includes rebilled costs) that you conservatively expect during the year (fiscal or calendar). You can easily reduce the budgeting process to quarterly or monthly increments.

Your actual costs for individual expense categories may vary from these percentage guidelines. However, stray too far above these suggested cost-to-income percentages and your bottom line results will be more bleak than you would like.

Monitor your actual costs against these guidelines on a regular basis, at least quarterly, preferably monthly. Change budgeted dollar figures as your income and expense projections change.

A good way to prepare your first budget is to break down the previous year's expenses into the categories listed here and use that not only as a guide in preparing a 12-month budget, but as an indication of where better cost controls may be needed.

TRACKING PROFITABILITY

To keep your firm moving forward, you need information on two types of profitability; overall agency results and individual client profitability.

FIGURE 12.1. Suggested Annual Firm Budget

Expenses		Percent of Projected Income
Salaries and Benefits	50	(Over 55% and you're in big trouble!)
Travel and Entertainment	2	(Nonbillable client expenses)
New Business Development	1	(2 or 3% may be more realistic with a very active new business program.)
Unbilled (Mistakes!)	1	(Expect, plan for them!)
Operating Expenses (Rent, utilities, telephone, maintenance, messenger, depreciation, etc.)	13	(Break out individual expense categories. Keep rent within 7-10% of income.)
General and Administration (Stationery, supplies, insurance, postage, dues and subscriptions, employee recruiting)	4	(Break out individual expense categories)
Payroll Taxes	4	(Depends on local rates)
Total salaries and expenses	75	(Attainable!)
Pre-tax profit	25	(Nirvana!)

Some years ago, I asked the general manager of a national firm's Chicago office whether his firm tracked individual client profitability. He said he didn't need such information because he knew that his office was profitable.

Contrast that misguided opinion with a letter from the president of a West Coast firm: "At your suggestion, our CFO developed hard data on profitability per client. We've since resigned seven accounts that were too small or were a pain. That allowed us to take one of our best people and assign her to a large account where she's doing a great job."

Here is a compelling truth: Just because your firm or office is profitable does not mean that all of your clients are profitable or as profitable as they could be. There may be leaks in the bucket!

Tracking the profitability of both your agency and each client–and doing something about problems in both areas–should be a monthly priority.

There are only four basic factors that need to be considered in tracking individual client profitability: income; salary costs (the actual cost to you of the time invested by employees in serving a client, whether the time is actually billed to the client or not); non-overhead expenses incurred on behalf of the client that cannot be rebilled; and your firm's overhead percentage.

Hourly salary costs are determined by dividing the total cost of an individual's annual salary and benefits by the total number of hours for which he or she is paid annually. For example, 40 hours a week equals 2,080 hours a year.

As we've noted previously, your firm's overhead percentage can be determined by dividing your total overhead costs (including nonchargeable staff salaries) by your total annual direct salary costs. Generally, your overhead percentage will range between 80 to 100 percent of salaries depending on how well you control costs.

Each month, multiply the hourly salary costs of all the people who worked on an account by the total number of hours charged against that client by each person (whether or not billed to the client). That will give you the total salary cost for each client for the month. (In this case only, don't worry about unbillable time; that is, the number of hours that staff members neither charge against or bill to clients.)

Next, multiply each client's salary costs by your overhead percentage. That will give you the expense overhead cost to be borne by each client. Each client carries the same overhead percentage. For example, $24,000 in salary costs times an 85 percent overhead percentage equals $20,400 in overhead costs to be applied to that account. You also should factor in other nonrebillable client costs such as travel, entertainment and any client-oriented vendor costs that cannot be rebilled to a client.

When you subtract the sum of salary costs and overhead expense share, plus miscellaneous client costs, from each client's gross income, you will arrive at profit or loss.

Here are two examples of the process:

Monthly Income	Salary/Benefit Costs	Overhead @ 85%	Total	Profit	Profit Percent
$10,000	$6,000	$5,100	$11,100	($1,100)	(LOSS)
$10,000	$5,000	$4,250	$9,250	$750	7.5

NOTE: There are several ways to shrink salary costs and increase profits: reduce the number of hours charged against a client but not billed; reduce the number of hours billed against a flat fee; or reduce the number of more costly hours invested in a client by more expensive senior employees.

Quality standards and client service needs must, of course, always be your highest priority. However, remember that you earn the most profit when the most highly competent, least costly employees do most of the work. In addition, if the overhead percentage in the second example above rose to 95 percent, the profit on the account would drop to $250. That's a 67 percent drop in operating profit because of a 10 percent increase in overhead costs. Factor that difference into your firm's "numbers." The result should be strong motivation for controlling overhead costs.

Tracking client profitability can be computerized either by using a software program that you or a consultant develop, by adapting Lotus 1-2-3 or by using software such as Adman® or MAS-90® that do it automatically.

Ask your accountant, financial officer or a computer consultant to recommend or design a computer program that will track and report both overall agency profitability and the profit or loss on individual clients.

RECOVERING CLIENT REBILLABLES

A PR firm principal (a relatively inexperienced one) asked, "Is it worth the time involved to bill clients back for expenses like telephone, copies, publications, messenger and fax charges?" Simple answer: yes!

It's always worth billing all reasonable expenses back to clients. Either track the exact costs (can be largely automated) or charge a percentage of the time bill to cover such costs. (A Chicago firm adds 5 percent to each bill to cover "miscellaneous postage, copies, telephone costs." Large mailings or copy runs are billed separately.)

Charging expenses back to clients adds cash directly to your bottom line. For example, how many copies do you make monthly? Only 2,000 copies per month charged to clients at ten cents each puts $2,400 back into your pocket annually and helps pay for your copier.

Some firms also charge clients for stationery with a price list for letterhead, memo paper, second sheets and envelopes.

Occasionally, there may be a question as to whether an item is an agency or client expense. For example, if you take a client to lunch, that's obviously the agency's expense. However, if you take both a client and an editor to lunch, that's the client's expense. (You probably won't get anyone to admit that when they take a client to lunch, they eat the cost, but bill the client an extra half hour that day to cover the lunch cost. But it happens.)

Remember, there is no such thing as a free lunch. Rule of thumb: Anything you do or spend on behalf of the client gets billed.

ELIMINATING WRITE-OFFS

The time that employees invest in client programs but which, for any number of reasons, can't be billed to a client can make a really sour impression on your bottom line.

Let's say, for example, that last month your billable fee income was $100,000. You had $50,000 (50 percent) in salary costs, including your own, and $35,000 (35 percent) in operating expenses, leaving an operating profit of $15,000. Pretty good, you say.

But what about the $5,000 in time and/or out-of-pocket costs that you couldn't bill to clients and had to write off? This is money that would have gone directly to your bottom line, increasing your operating profit to $20,000.

To generate that same $20,000 in operating profit the hard way, you would need to bill clients an additional $33,000 in fee income. (Fifteen percent of $133,000 is about $20,000.) It should be obvious that it is far easier to eliminate $5,000 in write-offs than to generate $33,000 in new income.

As we've noted before, writing off unbillable time or expenses—because of sloppy budgeting, human carelessness or over-investment of staff time—is one of the biggest single contributors to lower-than-possible PR firm profits.

Such gaffes not only take money out of your pocket, but also reduce the amount of cash available for employee salaries, benefits and bonuses. That fact alone should make staff members pay attention when you talk about the importance of reducing or, even better, eliminating write-offs.

Sometimes you may need to invest time in nonbillable client service. New-client-start-up or staff education can result in legitimate write-offs. But don't over-do it.

However, don't get so enthusiastic about over-servicing that you have trouble backing down after the first few months, particularly on a flat-fee client. Don't put up with employees who can't or won't work efficiently and effectively. (One individual getting away with doggin' it can make everyone else wonder why they're running so hard.)

Make sure that projects are budgeted accurately. Train staff people how to budget. Consider installing a computer budgeting system with on-line historical data and a standard budgeting form that contains all the elements of any project.

Make sure that employees understand exactly how much time has been budgeted to complete projects. Encourage and train people to complete work within budget and to know when to stop work.

Hold staff members responsible for careless mistakes or inaccurate or incomplete budgeting. Show employees the negative impact that write-offs have on the amount of bonus money available. Make it clear that every dollar lost through write-offs directly reduces the bonus dollars in their pockets.

Most important, make the elimination or drastic reduction of write-offs a personal priority! Do not permit employees, even senior people, to write off significant sums unless they have an excellent reason and your written approval. (Any write-off over $100 demanded my personal approval and a darn good reason.) When it comes time for bonuses, reward those who keep write-offs under control. (A West Coast firm, with a severe write-off problem largely because of over-servicing clients, based its bonus plan for senior people one year on rewards for reducing write-offs.)

Remember, it's a lot easier to boost your profits by eliminating write-offs than it is to earn increased income to produce the same result. Once you've generated income, it's a shame to pour it down the drain needlessly through carelessness, inefficiency, stupidity or lack of management concern and attention.

PROFILE 13

DAVID PAINE, PRESIDENT, PAINE & ASSOCIATES, COSTA MESA, CA

"We believe that the various elements of our business–our people, management, clients, suppliers and profit–all need to be given equal consideration; there has to be synergy between all the elements as the company moves forward and makes decisions about itself. This unique philosophy of doing business enables us to attract and serve clients well, attract and retain top talent, maintain very high levels of employee morale and minimize employee turnover," according to Paine.

With seven years of major PR firm experience under his belt, Paine started his firm in 1986 with five clients and $179,000 income the first year. Today, the firm has 33 clients, 35 employees, $4 million in income and a reputation as one of the country's best managed PR firms.

However, in the early years, Paine says he made such mistakes as: "Putting growth ahead of profit. Hiring people without proper diligence to ensure that they would be a good fit and contribute to the quality of the organization. And allowing the firm to run me, instead of managing the firm."

Advice for agency principals: "Be prepared to see your job change from practitioner to business manager. Be ready when it does by taking courses in business and human resource management. Don't just shoot from the hip or lip. That's what kills many growing agencies. Principals in firms like ours simply are not adequately skilled as business managers."

Chapter 13

Client Budgeting

Three of the most important elements of good client service are strategic thinking, creativity and budgeting. Often, budgeting gets 10 percent of the attention and causes 90 percent of the problems. Accurate budgeting requires careful planning, awareness of project variables, consideration of staff experience and skills and close attention to production details. And, most important, careful attention to the client's needs.

Conversely, while individual agencies may apply certain rules of thumb, there are very few guidelines that can be applied to all budgeting situations. Moreover, budgeting is seldom taught; it is usually learned by doing.

THE CLIENT'S NEEDS

Sears Roebuck and Co. PR executive Ron Culp told an audience of Chicago PR counselors:

"We view the client-agency relationship as a matter of complete mutual trust. Every budgeting problem that has ever arisen has been the result of a breakdown of that relationship."

There are three ways to destroy a good client relationship, Culp said:

1. Surprise the client, even in routine matters. In budgeting, this includes everything from underestimating to over-promising. Agencies should budget precisely, realistically and completely. Clients hate to see "TBD" (To Be Determined) in a proposed budget, Culp said.

2. Confuse the client by changing the game plan unexpectedly so that it impacts on costs and the budgets. Always involve the client in the decision process if circumstances make a change necessary that could impact on the budget. Culp advised agencies to provide as much detailed budget information as the client needs.

3. Cheat the client or appear to do so. The direct way to cheat, of course, is to bill the client for services or goods not performed or provided. The indirect approach, Culp said, is to add secondary vendor markups without the client's approval. Other ways to cheat the client are to: (1) operate on the theory that if it is in the budget, we should spend it; (2) consider that a contingency fund is available for day-to-day projects; and (3) propose or adjust budgets based on the perceived depth of the client's pockets.

From a speech by Ron Culp on client budgeting to the PRSA Counselors Group. Reprinted with permission.

SURPRISES KILL A BUDGET

When preparing a budget, you can never plan too much or pay too much attention to details. Here are two horror stories from the files of a national public relations agency.

Horror Story #1

To introduce a new food product, the agency planned to send samples of the product to food editors across the country so they could taste the frozen yogurt, at that time a new supermarket freezer category.

Unfortunately, when budgeting for the shipment of the samples, the agency was not aware and did not plan for the fact that the product had a melting tolerance of just five degrees. As a result, the product had to be packed in special containers that could accommodate dry ice and still meet air express regulations. The actual cost doubled budget projections. The budget melted but the product didn't.

Horror Story # 2

Although the agency had budgeted for the client to exhibit at a major trade show, no one knew that the exhibit was scheduled to be used at another show that ended two days before the start of their show. To make sure that the booth was at the convention site on time, the agency had to Federal Express a 10' x 20' booth. The shipping charges alone were $8,000. The booth looked great, but the budget looked terrible.

Moral: Surprises kill a budget! Always ask the right questions and then ask them again.

THE TEN BIGGEST BUDGETING PITFALLS

Here are the ten biggest budgeting pitfalls, according to Jerry Murray, former President, Ruder Finn/Chicago. Make sure that you avoid them.

1. Underestimating the time and manpower required;
2. Wanting to look good for a client or superior and purposely low-balling projected costs;
3. Misrepresenting a project to vendors and receiving incorrect cost projections;
4. Budgeting for a project without thinking the whole project through;
5. Not informing the client of budget problems until *after* the project is well underway or completed;
6. Not taking the time with a client at the beginning of the project to fully explain all the expected expenses and the exact components of the project;
7. Identifying a good opportunity during the project and not asking the client for more money to take advantage of the opportunity. Either trying to squeeze the opportunity in the budget, or passing it up;
8. Setting unrealistic timetables that cause you to put in overtime and/or over-staff a project;
9. Not budgeting for contingencies; and

10. Not giving complete budget information to all members of the account team.

MOST COMMON BUDGETING PROBLEMS

Of these pitfalls, agency principals say that the three most common and most serious budgeting problems are:

1. Under-Budgeting

Deliberately under-budgeting or low-balling because you are afraid that you might frighten or even lose the client if the projected cost is too high. In most cases, such concerns are unrealistic.

Clients can always find someone who will work cheaper than your firm, if that's what they want. On the other hand, it's important to apply what Lou Williams, President, L. C. Williams and Associates, Chicago calls "a sense of anticipation": being able to anticipate the cost level that will make the client's ears turn red . . . and not exceeding that level.

To stay within a realistic budget, you can reduce the scope of the program or give the client a selection of over-budget items that can be substituted for elements included in the budget. Warning: Don't be tempted to squeeze the budget just to get the business.

2. Faulty Time Estimates

Failure to accurately estimate how long it will take to complete a project or a program is different from deliberately under-budgeting to get a job or not anger a client. Both of these approaches are bound to result in either having to write off the cost overage or ask the client for more money–neither of which is a pleasant experience.

3. Incomplete Budgets

Forgetting important elements of the budget, such as postage or shipping costs or agency markup on production costs. It's very embarrassing to have to ask a client for more money because you forgot to include a production cost in the budget. But it hurts worse to have to eat your mistake. A little embarrassment can make up for a lot of red ink.

THE BUDGETING PROCESS

Budgeting ought to be really simple. There are only two things that you have to worry about: how much time will it take to complete a project or a program; and how much will the client have to pay for out-of-pocket costs and internal agency expenses? Doesn't that sound easy? If only it was.

Budgeting for out-of-pocket costs can and should be relatively simple. As long as you provide accurate and complete information, you can usually rely on vendors for accurate cost estimates. And as long as you remember to include all possible out-of-pocket expenses in your budget, you're home free. Estimating the amount of staff time that will be required to complete a project or program is a different kettle of fish.

A critical factor in preparing a budget is the level of experience and skill of the person or persons who will actually do the work. Unfortunately, the person developing the budget usually has more experience than the person or persons who will carry out the project and can do the job faster. That can cause problems.

Should the senior person budget for as much time as he or she knows it would take them to personally complete the assignment? Should he try to guess how much time it will take a junior person, or should he ask the junior person how much time he or she thinks will be needed?

Like so many things in the agency business, the right answer is an average: an estimate of the average time that it should take a relatively experienced person to complete the project. And experience will usually tell you what that ought to be.

But then there are the variables: those things that you can't plan for but that will happen as sure as Sullivan's Law decrees that if something can go wrong, it will.

Unfortunately, it is very difficult to teach people how to budget because of the huge variety of projects that a firm can be asked to handle, some of which it may never have handled before, and the possible variables that can affect costs.

Individuals often learn to budget on their own through experience, and trial and error. A better way to learn is to work with an experienced person, either in a client or classroom situation. Many firms have written guidelines, based on past experience, that can be very useful, although not infallible. It follows then that the more experience you have, the better your judgement and instincts will be. And the easier it will be for you to produce accurate budgets.

The most practical approach to budgeting is to apply the averages and add a safety factor. Estimate the average cost of specific projects, and then add a fudge factor for variables and unforeseen circumstances. Or as one agency principal said, "If I think an article ought to cost $2,000, I'll budget it for $2,500, just to be sure." On the other hand, you could safely budget ten articles at an average of $2,000 each, because some of the articles will cost more and some less than $2,000 and the averages will work out.

HOW TO DEVELOP A BUDGET

Translate your personal experience into an estimate of the time required to complete specific projects; news releases, brochures, special events, etc. Consider the required investment of time as if it was being expended consecutively and continuously.

You have a press conference to be budgeted. How much time will be required for management/supervision, research, brainstorming, planning, writing, photography, client approvals, rewrite, media contact, travel, event and production supervision and reporting and merchandising results? Consider the skill level of people who may be involved. How much time will be required for client meetings and executive counseling? Then consider the agency's experience or the average cost for similar projects, if such information is available.

Multiply the number of estimated per-project and total hours by your average hourly rate. Add another 20 to 25 percent to this sum to allow for Sullivan's Law.

When estimating production costs, include such out-of-pocket costs as:

- Design and illustration;
- Free-lancers and consultants;
- Photography;
- Printing;
- Mailing and handling;
- Food and refreshments;
- Audio visual material;
- Travel;
- Model and/or spokesperson fee;
- Equipment rental; and
- Markup (if any).

Include such agency expenses as:

- Telephone (including data base search charges);
- Fax;
- Copies;
- Clipping and video service;
- Publication subscriptions;
- Postage, shipping, messenger; and
- Editorial and client entertainment.

COMPUTER BUDGETING

Admittedly, the budgeting process described here is little more than a few homemade, hand-me-down, shot-in-the-dark techniques based on hopefulness and educated guesses. But that's the way agencies have done it for years. The majority still do.

However, there is a better way. More and more firms are installing a computer budgeting system.

Computer budgeting consists of an on-line client budgeting form and a historical data base containing documentation of agency cost experience in past activity. The form offers a detailed listing of all the optional time and production cost factors for a variety of specific projects or programs. (See Benjamin Group example in Appendix D, pp. 234-235.)

The historical database contains actual or average costs for various projects completed over a period of time. (In some systems, this data base is updated every time client invoices are prepared.)

The data base serves as a starting point for budget development, provides a standard, disciplined approach to budgeting and helps remind practitioners of factors to be included in the budget. It also helps train people to budget by providing comparisons for budget accuracy.

In a typical system, the practitioner accesses a budget form for the project type he or she is working on, for example, a ten-city media tour. On his monitor, he sees all the possible elements of such a tour–planning, writing, supervision, media contact, etc.–with blanks for the estimated time required to complete each element of the project.

The practitioner fills in the blanks and enters the name of the practitioner or title (account executive, account supervisor) who will likely do the work. The system automatically computes the cost of each element and the total project cost based on the amount of estimated time and the hourly rate of the persons/titles specified. If the practitioner wants to refer to the agency's past experience in the type of project that he is budgeting, he calls up historical data in a monitor window. A complete budget estimate is printed out and can be submitted to the client.

Data Base Categories

Your data base may contain the following historical data:

Writing	releases, feature articles, technical articles, op-ed, radio/TV scripts;
Media Relations	media list preparation, editorial contact, press conference, media tour;
Special Events	sports, civic, political, local, regional, national, trade show;
Publications; irregular	annual/quarterly report, brochures–multiple page/multiple color/varied quantity;
Publications; regular	newsletter, newspaper, magazine–multiple page/multiple color/varied quantity;
Audio visual	video, film, slides, desktop publishing;

Research	internal, external, major, minor, mail, telephone, mall intercept, local, regional, national;
Planning	research, brainstorming, meetings, writing, critique, rewrite;
Administration	paperwork, reports, travel, review publications, billing;
Production costs, expenses, taxes	with/without markup, out-of-state shipment;
Contingency	10 to 15 percent.

Computer Budgeting Benefits

Installing a computer budgeting system may require a significant investment of time to compile and enter the data base information. However, such a system offers a number of benefits:

1. Saves time–why reinvent the wheel?
2. Provides a common approach to budgeting.
3. Improves budgeting accuracy.
4. Can be customized for individual situations.
5. Helps train staff members.

AND IN THE END

Three broad rules will help guide you through the budgeting labyrinth:

1. Always get the client's approval of the budget in writing or confirm a budget decision in a written conference report.
2. Never invest any time on the client's behalf until the budget is approved.
3. Clients will almost never object if you come in under budget.

PROFILE 14

STEVEN PARKER, PRESIDENT, CORPORATE COMMUNICATIONS LTD., HALIFAX, NS CANADA

In 1977, six years out of college, Parker started a PR firm that generated $42,000 in income the first year. Jump 17 years; Parker now heads a $10 million integrated communications firm with three offices, 240 employees and $3.5 million of PR income (making it the second largest Canadian PR firm).

"Our market is smaller than many major U.S. cities," says Parker. "So our number one rule for getting business is to keep the business we have. We still have our first client, Maritime Life Assurance, as well as our second and third clients. We build business brick by brick with a focus on professionalism and service rather than on new clients."

Parker first integrated his firm–combining advertising and PR under the same umbrella–to gain the mass needed to hire top level people. Early in 1994, however, specialties were divided into divisions and PR became a profit center. "This latter move came because the firm needed a higher level of specialists," says Parker, "as well as to improve the firm's focus on worldwide quality and assign executives responsibility for clearly accountable business functions."

Despite its seeming isolation, the firm attracts top professional talent both locally and from other parts of Canada. In addition, Mt. Saint Vincent University–the first Canadian university to graduate PR-degreed students–provides a good local supply of junior people.

Chapter 14

Recruiting, Training, and Retaining Employees

It's true; your inventory goes down in the elevator every night and, hopefully, comes back up in the morning. Efficiently and effectively recruiting, training and motivating people are keys to building and maintaining your talent inventory.

Public relations firm principals complain that finding and keeping qualified employees at a reasonable cost–particularly at more experienced levels–is a major challenge. The amount of business available to PR firms, coupled with a shortage of good people, puts great importance on sophisticated recruiting techniques, supportive training methods and superlative motivational and morale-boosting efforts.

RECRUITING GOOD EMPLOYEES

Here are eight strategies to help make your search for competent practitioners more cost effective and productive:

1. Use Employment or Search Firms . . . Selectively

A $30,000 account executive, hired through an employment agency or executive recruiter, can cost you $9,000 or more in fees, and then be unprofitable for months while he or she learns to become productive or billable.

On the other hand, there undoubtedly will be occasions when a good professional recruiter can find a well-qualified practitioner or special-skills professional either locally or in another part of the country, when you can't or don't have time to conduct a proper search. You will need to decide whether your time constraints are so severe or your staff requirements so urgent or specific that you must look to an outside source. In such cases, the investment, while hefty, can be worthwhile.

If you don't use an outside source, however, how do you find the people you need? There are a number of good methods, some of which are more long-range than others, but all of which will pay off.

2. Make It Easy for Good People to Find You

Aim everything you do at three groups of people: your clients, prospects . . . and future employees.

Become highly visible. Promote your firm in ways that potential employees will notice. Get people talking about you and your agency. Become involved in professional associations. Make speeches, appear on panels, write articles and announce your new business wins locally and nationally. Make sure that the public relations community is aware of your firm's growth and stature. Growth is attractive to prospective employees as well as to prospective clients.

3. Create a Pleasant and Satisfying Workplace Atmosphere

To reduce turnover as well as attract new people, establish and nurture a workplace ambiance that ordains your firm with the reputation as a good place to work.

Here are some things you can do to help build that kind of reputation:

- Compensate employees fairly;
- Push responsibility and authority down to the lowest possible level;
- Involve staff members in as many aspects of the agency as possible;
- Provide opportunities for personal and professional growth;
- Recognize good work and reward top performers;
- Conduct regular and meaningful performance reviews;

- Support staff development with training, seminars and professional conferences;
- Hold staff lunches and outings;
- Be realistic and reasonable in staff productivity requirements;
- Inform employees about agency, client and new business developments;
- Be cordial and caring in dealing with staff members and do everything possible to enhance staff members' sense of self-worth. Word spreads about the good places to work as well as the "sweat shops."

4. Tap Professional Resources

Get to know your fellow agency principals; they usually will be willing to refer qualified employee candidates whom they can't use at the moment. Ask them to refer people with specific experience to you, not just "anyone you don't need." Reciprocate by referring candidates to other principals. Utilize professional association job banks and offer a reward to staff members who refer new employees (if the new employee stays at least three months).

5. Build a Resume File

Don't discard resumes, particularly if the individual appears to have potential. You may need a specific individual some time after you first receive his or her resume and they may still be available. Maintain a file by experience-level categories such as graduate, mid-level, senior, or by job backgrounds such as packaged goods, high tech, food, or business-to-business. This will help you locate potential candidates quickly without searching the entire file.

Keep the file current by regularly deleting resumes more than two years old. Chances are, the individual has moved on by then or rigor mortis has set in. If you should happen to contact someone through an old resume and find that they have already changed jobs, make a note of the new position. You may be able to hire an individual as much as a year or two after you first receive their resume.

6. Be Available

Make time to interview people regularly, even if you have no openings or are not looking for someone with their background. In particular, talk to recent or upcoming graduates as often as you can. They need encouragement and experience handling interviews. Interviewing a near or new graduate will help keep you current on the availability of entry level people and the caliber and curriculum of public relations education. It will also build your file of potential employees and help create a good reputation for your firm.

7. Use Interns Productively

Colleges and universities are an excellent source of part-time or short-time staff members. Provide internships to as many talented university students–not necessarily all PR majors–as you can handle productively and profitably at one time. Internships will help build a backlog of semi-professional individuals who are grounded in and enthusiastic about your firm and who may qualify for full-time employment when they graduate.

Use interns part-time during the school year and full-time during the summer. Students can be productive if they have 15 to 20 hours available a week. Pay interns a reasonable salary ($7-10 per hour) and charge their time fairly to clients ($25-35 per hour).

Consider appointing one of your better young account executives on a rotating basis as intern supervisor to schedule the interns' time, act as a mentor and monitor their training under your guidance. The interns will relate well to the younger person and the account executive will gain supervision experience. You may also want to let the intern supervisor recruit and hire interns with your final approval. It will be valuable experience for the intern supervisor with little exposure to your firm.

Internships should be productive both for you and the student. Assign interns to meaningful tasks within their capabilities. Don't limit them to clerical assignments or pro bono projects that do not provide realistic training in client service or insight into the reality of everyday productivity demands.

Given the proper supervision, talented interns can handle lower level responsibilities well. This not only gives the intern practical training, but spares your more senior people from handling "grunt work" and ensures that the intern is modestly profitable. The intern's enthusiastic report to fellow students or professors about his or her satisfying and stimulating sojourn in the outside world will help attract a continuing stream of good intern and graduate candidates.

While most prospective interns will be juniors or seniors, you may want to offer limited-duration (three month) internships to graduates with no commitment of a job at the end. However, require the graduate to commit to remain the entire internship. Keep track of good interns when they graduate, even if you can't use them at that time.

Let colleges and universities in your area know about your internship program. Send professors and intern program coordinators a persuasive description of your internship program that can be posted on school bulletin boards. Speak to university classes and work with student PR association chapters.

8. Advertise for People, but Don't Skimp

Don't believe the old saw that "good people don't answer ads." They do, but you must advertise persuasively and in the open.

Place an attractive, well-written, decent-size display ad in the Sunday business news section of the best major newspaper in your area. Identify your firm. If you are not in a large, metropolitan area, use a newspaper published in the nearest big city. For instance, the *Chicago Tribune* pulls well in Wisconsin.

Don't skimp by inserting a few lines of anonymous type in the classified "Help Wanted" section. Blind ads are not as effective as signed ads; they generally attract fewer, well-qualified applicants. (In addition, people may be concerned that the unidentified agency is their own firm.)

Using this approach, you can reach and attract better qualified people who may not even be looking for a new job. Many PR practitioners habitually read the Sunday newspaper business section, including the "Executive Careers" display ads. They may not read the classified ad section.

I tested this theory by running the same attractive, signed display ad in both the classified and business news sections of the *Chicago*

Tribune on succeeding Sundays. The response by better qualified people from the business news section was almost double the response from the classified section.

In your ad, sell your firm (remember, prospects also read the Sunday newspaper) and the opportunities offered. Describe experience and skill requirements. Specify that applicants should not telephone but should write you a letter selling themselves. Individuals who can sell themselves well in a letter usually make good public relations professionals and, in particular, fit well in an agency atmosphere.

Answer all application letters quickly with a form letter that you personally sign. You may want to use several different form letters, depending on the applicants' experience and potential. One of these candidates may later become an employee, prospect or client. Make a good impression now. However, ash can resumes that are not accompanied by a letter. Someone who can't follow instructions well enough to write a letter (and not telephone) probably will not be able to follow job instructions.

Don't worry about receiving a flood of mail that will take too much time to read. In a few seconds, you can scan the first two paragraphs of a letter and decide whether you want to read more or perhaps talk to the individual. A typical well-written ad in a major metropolitan newspaper, for example, can produce several hundred responses. Out of this, you should get at least six or seven viable candidates and another 30 to 50 resumes that you will want to file.

There are other advertising avenues; ads in out-of-town locations, with a good supply of the kind of people that you need, can be effective. National publications, such as Public Relations Society of America publications, *Ad Age, PR Services Report* and *Adweek* can generate qualified applicants, but you may find that most of the respondents are from distant locations requiring heavy moving expenses. *The Wall Street Journal* pulls well when you are seeking senior people.

Over a ten-year period, during which I hired about 60 people, I used a placement firm only twice. All the rest of the new employees were attracted through metropolitan newspaper ads or came in unsolicited largely because of the firm's reputation as a good place to work.

Recruiting the right kind of people is a long-range proposition; a task that must be worked at constantly, not just when an opening suddenly occurs.

TRAINING, MOTIVATING AND RETAINING EMPLOYEES

Once you have hired good employees, do everything possible to prevent them from being lured away by better opportunities.

One of the most effective ways to motivate and retain good employees is to help them build a strong sense of their own self-worth. Make sure that employees understand that a public relations agency is one of the few places where an individual's personal and professional growth depends almost entirely on his or her personal capabilities and effort.

Corporations and other institutions tend to be highly structured within their public relations departments; starting at the top with a vice president/director and dropping vertically down the chain to the lowest denominator. The only way an individual can move up is usually when a more senior person leaves the company (and with corporate downsizing, the squeeze is even tighter). If you are the sole PR practitioner in a corporation, the chances are few for you to move into other areas of responsibility. However, as a PR agency grows, opportunities grow to match increased client income.

Teach employees that managing income–not working more hours–is the secret to increased responsibility and personal growth. There are only so many hours that an employee can work in a year and only so much income that he or she can generate personally.

The secret to individual personal growth is gaining increased responsibility for agency income. An employee can personally generate only about $125,000 to $150,000 annually in income. However, if an account executive is *responsible* for $400,000 in income, it follows that other employees must work for the account executive in order for the income to be generated.

People who are intelligent, highly motivated, interested in building client income and able to juggle multiple assignments will be excited and ultimately rewarded by this opportunity. This factor sets PR agencies apart from most other organizations in terms of professional and personal growth and increased compensation.

Training Employees

Helping employees improve their professional skills through organized training materials and programs will improve the level and quality of your firm's client service. It will also improve employee morale and help you retain valuable employees. Here are some suggested training ideas:

1. *Orientation/account management manual*–A typical manual, given to all new employees, contains information and guidance on agency policies and practices including:

   - *Program administration*–conference reports, status reports, and time accounting;
   - *Managing client money*–expense reports, purchase orders, supplier invoices, client and project job numbers;
   - *Miscellaneous procedures*–telephone system, computer and word processing systems, office supplies, travel arrangements, building access, proofreading system, filing system, document control system, media contact form, and style and graphics standards.

2. *Account start-up manual*–To help ensure proper start-up of service to a new client, the manual should outline general operating procedures. It should contain a comprehensive checklist of information and data required from a new client and a list of material (policies, manuals, marketing programs, etc.) required.

3. *Mentor system*–Junior and new employees are each assigned to a senior person who acts as the junior's mentor. Mentor and employee meet regularly, possibly for lunch at the agency's expense to discuss agency policies and procedures, client service matters, professional development and other matters concerning the junior person. Ideally, the mentor should not be assigned to any account that the junior works on so that the junior will feel free to discuss sensitive matters.

4. *In-house seminars*–Specialized professional training provided either by a senior agency employee or by an outside consultant. (For example, this writer conducts all-day, in-house account management seminars for agency staff members.)

5. *Outside seminars, conferences, professional associations*–Encourage employees to join and participate in the Public Relations Society of America's local chapter. (You should join PRSA's Counselors Academy.) Many agencies pay employees' professional organization membership dues and allow expense account charges for lunches, local meetings and national conferences. (Several times a year, I put all account executives' names in a hat and drew one to attend a national or regional conference.)
6. *Account involvement*–Provide as much authority and responsibility to employees as quickly as possible, but with senior oversight.

Retaining Employees

There are many opportunities for PR firm principals to gain satisfaction from their job. You will be able to name yours. If you are lucky, one of those will be low or no employee turnover. Few things hurt a firm more than losing fine professional employees–clients hate it–after investing considerable time, effort and cash in recruiting and training them.

I was one of the lucky ones. In 15 years of managing three successful public relations firms, I lost very few employees to better opportunities. In fact, only one person in all that time moved to another PR agency on his own volition.

If you would have asked people why they stayed, the answer might have been simply, "I like it here."

There is no one reason–beyond the generic "I like it here"–to account for extended employee tenure. Perhaps, the most important incentive lies with the agency principal. The principal sets the tone and flavor for the entire organization. You are the spark, the personality and the pace car for your agency.

If you are fair, open, candid and nonthreatening, employees will respond positively. If your counsel to clients is creditable, your professional skills admired and your new business successes appreciated, the examples you set will drive your agency forward. If you are very talented, yet keep a lock on your ego, staff members will follow suit. If you keep your fingers out of the soup, staff members will grow professionally and creatively. If you take your work seriously, but laugh at yourself, a sweeping sense of humor will pervade the agency. If you believe in working hard, but having fun while doing it, employees will function smoothly under day-to-day job pressure and clients will bask in service satisfaction.

If you ascribe high productivity as a mark of professional excellence, others will pride themselves in their ability to generate agency income. If you encourage employees to cross client lines and seek assignments on other accounts, home economists can write industrial case histories to stay billable and traverse into new spheres. If you refuse to grant sovereignty over individuals to second level managers, demanding that they teach and encourage rather than rule, fiefdoms will run fallow and professional independence will flourish.

If you are aware of individual achievement and lavish laurels on individuals, both achievers and nonachievers will be spurred to greater heights. (Half of my agency's bulletin board was designated a "Glory Board." Employees were encouraged to place laudatory descriptions there of other employee's accomplishments; a client cover story, a major feature placement, client praise, etc. For special exploits, a special ceremony was conducted at a staff lunch or meeting and a large glittering star was hung around the celebrant's neck.)

If your door remains open and you walk the halls regularly, people will open up to you and speak their minds. If you foster a strong sense of confidence and self-worth among staff members, practitioners will be encouraged to stretch beyond the mundane and will reach for the top of the mountain; risk-taking will be a normal, expected moment in their business day.

I like to think that I was all of these things. We had little staff turnover.

PERFORMANCE REVIEWS–STAFF AND MANAGEMENT

Staff members need to know where they stand with you. Each employee should receive an annual written review of his or her performance. Some agencies tie performance reviews in with salary reviews. Others conduct performance reviews on the individual's annual anniversary, but award salary increases on a calendar year basis so that all increases are effective on the same date.

The reality is that employees expect salary increases to be tied into performance reviews. I have always felt that this method resulted in higher morale than separating the two processes for accounting convenience. (When you tell someone they're doing a good job, they want to see visible evidence in their paycheck.)

Whichever method you use, be sure that employees understand your policy.

HOW AM I DOING?

Employees may know how you rate their performance, but have you ever asked your staff to *evaluate your performance* as a manager and leader? Have you ever asked employees what they expect from you or what changes they'd like to see in your firm's operation?

Try it. Ask employees to rank your management performance on a 1 to 10 (10 highest) scale in a number of areas. To enhance survey credibility, you may want to have an outside party, such as your accountant, tally the results. Staff members also are likely to be more candid in a confidential survey that does not reveal their identities.

Two caveats: To make this work, it's vital that you: (1) *discuss the survey results* with your staff in a group meeting, no matter how negative or positive the results may be; and (2) do everything possible *to correct any problems* revealed by the survey. If you don't take these two follow-up steps, the survey is a waste of everyone's time.

Ask your employees to rank you in these 25 areas:

HOW AM I DOING?

Responsibility   Ranking (1 - 10)
1. Provides instructions and information
   necessary to complete assignments?   _____
2. Clearly outlines expectations and objectives?   _____
3. Provides training necessary for growth; is a
   good teacher?   _____

4. Provides opportunities for growth; challenges
   staff members to grow and assume additional
   responsibility?   _____
5. Encourages innovation?   _____
6. Encourages alternate ideas; permits and
   encourages disagreement on creativity
   and client service; does not always insist
   on "doing it my way"?   _____
7. Provides responsibility and authority to
   complete assignments; keeps hands
   out of the soup to a reasonable degree?   _____
8. Is open and available for discussion of
   business or personal problems?   _____
9. Keeps staff informed about agency status/
   problems/opportunities/successes?   _____
10. Promotes a congenial, comfortable, collegial
    working atmosphere; believes in having fun?   _____
11. Is realistic about billable time goals?   _____
12. Discusses office policy or procedure changes
    with staff and asks for input?   _____
13. Supports staff in client discussions and
    disagreements whenever possible?   _____
14. Is fair and realistic in criticism of staff
    performance?   _____
15. Criticizes and/or reprimands individuals
    in private?   _____
16. Displays a calm, even temperament most of
    the time; is short on ego?   _____
17. Has established a good reputation for this
    agency in the public relations community?   _____
18. Is a skilled PR practitioner (when he/she
    needs to be); has professional skills that
    I respect?   _____
19. Respects others' experience and skills?   _____
20. Pays competitive salaries?   _____
21. Provides competitive benefits?   _____
22. Has established good, practical
    administrative systems and procedures?   _____

23. Deals fairly and equally well with both
    male and female staff members? _____
24. Has made this a good place to work? _____
25. Is a good overall manager? _____

Please complete the following:

1. The most demeaning, annoying and/or humiliating rule/procedure/form/regulation/policy that I have to live with is:

_____

_____

2. If I could change only one thing about this firm, I would:

_____

_____

Now See How You did

To see how employees evaluate your management ability, add up the scores for each question and average them. Compile individual answers to the two questions above. Then rank your performance on this scale:

HOW AM I DOING?

8 - 10	Excellent –	Apply for your halo.
6 - 7	Good –	Couldn't be much better.
4 - 5	Average –	Needs improvement.
1 - 3	Poor –	Why does anyone work for you?

Good luck! I hope you fare well in your staff's evaluation. But, if you don't, I hope you have the sense to do something about it!

PROFILE 15

ROBERT SCHENKEIN, PRESIDENT,
SCHENKEIN/SHERMAN PR, DENVER, CO

Two things distinguish Schenkein/Sherman from most other mid-size PR firms. First, the agency started in 1973 with $177,000 of PR income, evolved into a full service advertising and public relations agency (now called an integrated communications firm) and then–bucking a trend–spun off the advertising side. Schenkein stayed with the $1.5 million PR unit.

Second, few firms of its size have received as many regional and national awards for creativity. Example: Several Silver Anvils from the Public Relations Society of America and multiple awards, including the Gold CIPRA from *Inside PR* magazine for a Coors Brewing literacy program.

All was not so rosy in the early days. With no agency experience to guide him, Schenkein made mistakes. "I soloed on everything; hired a lot of rookies; did not have experienced backup; had no proactive marketing plan, waited for business to walk in the door; tended to accept any type of client and often stretched the agency too thin trying to keep up with the broad client base; did not build evaluation methodology into our programs; and should have joined a PR agency network earlier (a group of cooperative, non-competitive firms).

"Today, I'd work first for a large regional or national firm; hire experienced senior personnel sooner; join the PRSA Counselors Academy; and attract a highly qualified partner."

Chapter 15

Managing Expansion Problems
and Priorities

Anticipating and managing the priorities and problems that come with expansion could be compared to learning to ice skate. It's not as easy as it looks, but it's certainly as much fun as you expected . . . once you get the hang of it.

"A public relations firm is like a fish. If you're not moving ahead, people may think you're dying . . . or already dead," according to Paul Franson, President of Franson, Hagerty and Associates, a high tech public relations firm in San Jose, California and Washington, D.C.

On the other hand, if you move ahead too fast, with your eyes closed and no sense of direction, you may slam your nose on a rock. You may also:

1. Run yourself ragged;
2. Lose good people;
3. Lose clients; and
4. Lose money.

After surviving recessions, reduced or eliminated client budgets and disappointing new business pitches, as well as the joys and trauma of fast expansion, over a 25-year agency career, I learned that it is often as difficult to manage expansion as it is to cope with more negative aspects of the agency business. I also learned that following a few simple principles will guide you safely through to the promised payoff.

Careful planning, good backup people to manage and maintain quality client service, a solid business plan with well thought-out systems and procedures and enough cash or a good credit line ought to be your most important expansion priorities.

A survey of PR firm principals who have experienced fast expansion indicated that the primary problems and priorities of expansion revolve almost exclusively around two factors: people and systems.

Strangely enough, having enough funds to support expansion was not usually mentioned as an unsolvable or particularly difficult problem, assuming that the firm was able to establish a good credit line early on and paid consistent and concentrated attention to collecting receivables. It's also important that the principal not try to take all the gold out of the mine for himself or herself at the beginning but put money back into the business. One principal said, "If you are in this business for the short run, you are in for trouble."

A West Coast principal calculates that every new employee costs at least $15,000 for computers, furniture and other items, not to mention salary, before the new practitioner earns a cent for the firm. This firm exploded to more than 30 people and two offices in just under five years. The principal knows that she must be prepared for a serious cash outlay every time she thinks about adding people.

Another owner said, "Establish your credit line before you need it. Get the biggest line of credit you can. You may not think you need a credit line until one of your clients gets in trouble and pays you in 90 days instead of 45 and you have to make payroll. When you're expanding, you don't have time to figure out where you're going to get that next bit of cash that you need."

In almost every instance, the principals talked about the problems that a lack of good backup professionals–usually a number two person–caused during expansion. The biggest problem, as you might imagine, was poor quality control in client service. (On the other side, clients often complain that agencies spend too much time seeking new business and not enough serving their current clients.)

When expansion hits, principals are often spread too thin to pay attention to everything. A Northern California principal said, "I got too fragmented, lost control and had huge staff and client turnover." The owner finally solved his problem by hiring an experienced professional to back him up. Asked how he would handle expansion if he had it to do over again under similar circumstances, he said,

"First, I would find a super number two person to focus on running current business."

In another instance, a Midwest principal said his mistake was trying to find a senior person on the outside when he had good people inside who could have been promoted to greater responsibility.

A New York City principal said the key to managing expansion was knowing the capabilities and capacity of your present staff and being aware of how much additional business they could handle properly.

Another New York City principal noted that expansion forced him to trust his staff and learn to delegate . . . not too much and not too little.

Several principals recommended staying at least one person ahead all the time. In other words, having at least one more person on staff than your current business will support. Or, at the very least, keeping your networks warm and being aware of people who can be hired quickly when it becomes necessary to staff up. That means interviewing people regularly, even though you may not have an opening at the time, and building a good resume file.

All of this boils down to one rather obvious fact: if you don't invest early on in the right kind and number of senior people to help you manage growth, you are likely to encounter very rough times and could end up worse off than before you expanded. The best time to acquire or train your backup is before growth problems smother you.

The same philosophy applies to the installation of systems that you will need to manage expansion. Put your systems in place before you need them! That deserves repetition because it is so important. Put your administrative systems in place before you need them. It is much easier to install systems while you are small than to try to impose them when you are larger or trying to handle rapid growth. What kind of systems will you need?

To start with, a networked computer system. Accounting and time-keeping software that lets you automate time sheets, get out billing before the middle of the month and track agency and client profitability (see Chapter 9). And while you're at it, consider installing a computerized budgeting system that will help you efficiently develop accurate budgets for all those new clients.

An effective system to keep track of expenses to be billed back to clients is vital. As one agency principal said, "The more clients you have, the more money can dribble through your hands without the right systems. If you haven't caught on to the right systems when you have two or three clients, heaven help you when you have 15."

One principal even said that if he had to make a cash decision between people and systems, he probably would put his money into systems. Five years ago, this firm's computers were not networked. Staff members often had difficulty locating stored information. Information could not be shared easily between practitioners or support staff. Today, that principal says, "Networking my computers was the best investment I ever made."

Another principal said, "Systems saved us. We always had better systems than were absolutely needed at the time. We watched our numbers very closely and had a handle on profitability long before most agencies do. When we put a stamp on an envelope, we got 29 cents back from the client. We knew the number of hours our people billed and how that applied to clients. When we needed more sophisticated systems, we brought in a business manager."

Other systems that you will need when you expand that, perhaps, you could do without when you were smaller, include channels to communicate easily and efficiently with all employees (E-mail) and an organizational infrastructure that defines account management responsibilities. A New Jersey firm that grew from a four-person home-basement-office to an 11-person commercial office in less than a year encountered serious problems. Information was not flowing up from the account staff to management and the principal had trouble managing and maintaining client service quality control. An outside consultant helped the principal establish a management structure and a communication system that solved the problem.

You also should develop an orientation program and manual for new employees as well as an account start-up manual to define the standard procedures that must be gone through and the information and materials that are needed when beginning service to a new client (see Chapter 14).

Train your staff not only to serve clients properly but to manage accounts profitably. Too often, staff members, particularly younger employees, are totally committed to providing excellent client service, but don't pay enough attention to the agency's need to be profitable.

Office space is, of course, another problem that comes with expansion. Where are you going to put all the people you hire to handle all the new business? Most principals in the survey recommended always having slightly more space than you need at the moment, but not so much that rental costs become excessive. Doubling up in offices is possible, but seldom comfortable or efficient. Subletting excess space to a noncompetitor is an option. Two independent New York firms even share the same space.

How do you know when you're ready to expand? There are two ways; one based on projected income and the other on a more philosophical approach.

RESOURCE ALLOCATION MATRIX

Since expansion means new clients, new income and additional employees, a need exists to look ahead and project how all the new business is likely to impact on your staff requirements.

The Resource Allocation Matrix shown in Chapter 10 will help you accomplish this. Applying the Matrix will enable you to determine the number of people you are likely to need in the future based on the income you expect to generate both from current and new clients. Using this Matrix also will help you plan, assign, and balance work loads, balance income and avoid problems caused by the cyclical nature of the agency business. In addition, it will help keep average staff productivity high and provide guidelines for short- and long-term staff needs.

THE PHILOSOPHICAL APPROACH

A second way to determine whether you are ready to expand requires personal introspection and answers to some tough questions:

- Does the potential new business have substantial, long-range, profit potential or is it likely to be only a short burst?

- Is my credit line or cash flow good enough to support the additional cost of serving the new business before it becomes profitable?
- Do I have the right kind of people in place or available to manage expansion and maintain client service? Will I have to hire people?
- Do I have the systems in place or in development that I will need when we get bigger?

Probably the most difficult question to answer is a very personal one. Do I have to expand and do I want to? One principal warned, "The big message is . . . decide what you want to do. Don't let expansion be forced on you if you aren't ready or don't want it."

Expansion brings some special business considerations and personal demands that are less important when you're smaller. How much expansion can you handle? Be realistic about how much money you will need to expand and how much of your profit you want to use to expand. In reality, you're spending your take-home money.

Don't expand too fast. Determine what your revenue will be and what expenses and profits would be if you stay the same size. Your formulas are going to change radically when you grow.

Decide how big you want to be. Do you want your firm to have five people or 50 people? Sometimes, small firms win large accounts, are forced to hire additional people and, suddenly, are bigger than the principal wanted to be in the first place.

"If you don't decide what you want to do," one principal said, "the tail wags the dog, the owner feels victimized, employees feel like a ship without a captain or a rudder . . . and everyone is miserable."

Too often, a principal may not think about the impact of expansion on him or her. What it means to your personal and professional life in terms of the time you will have to spend with your family or do the kinds of things you like to do . . . including work with clients.

One of the biggest problems among small- and medium-size firms is reluctance or inability of the principal to separate himself or herself far enough from client service so that he or she has enough time to manage the business properly and make it grow profitably.

Be very clear about one thing. If you are to manage expansion properly and come out of it profitably and with your skin on, you will be required to do less client work and handle more administrative chores. That can be a real problem, particularly if you like to do client work and have trouble giving it up.

Expansion also brings with it a broader need to motivate other people. You may need to be careful about the image you project to your staff. One owner said that he had a habit of sighing to relax. He found this to be very cathartic. Unfortunately, he learned that staff members thought his sighs meant that the company was in trouble.

A top executive of a national PR firm feels that he must never display excessive happiness or unhappiness because of what he might inadvertently communicate to employees.

Where you are in your life also is an important expansion consideration. As one female principal put it, "If you feel young and energetic . . . no matter what your biological age . . . and are ready to kick butts and take names, that is the time to expand." (Note: This mother of two recommends not trying to expand while you are pregnant.)

So . . . if you're ready to kick butts and take names . . . go to it . . . and good luck.

PROFILE 16

WINNIE SHOWS, PRESIDENT, SMITH & SHOWS PR, MENLO PARK, CA

Ten years as a high school teacher, four years in high tech PR and a founding partner who offered both encouragement and business convinced Winnie Shows in 1984 that the Silicon Valley needed a high tech firm specializing in Unix and "open systems" clients. (Others, since proved wrong, advised her against such specialization.)

Contributing to the firm's growth to $712,000 income have been a strong direct marketing program and such innovative new business techniques as telemarketing. Shows now emphasizes a relaxed "go with the flow" management style ("I don't have to work so hard and I get bigger and better clients this way") and innovative "new age" employee practices.

Typical: A part-time employee runs personal errands for other employees several mornings a week; employees with school age children have flexible work schedules. "This relaxed approach has led to happier employees who take more responsibility for their behavior," Shows says.

There were early mistakes: "Not being on top of receivables; being too eager to please clients and over-servicing accounts; and not responding fast enough to business downturns."

Shows advises firm principals: "Have a sense of humor; maintain a personal life; exercise regularly; and consider taking up meditation. All this will keep your engines charged and enable you to work smarter."

Chapter 16

Crisis Planning for PR Firms

APRIL 1991–A workshop on crisis planning for public relations firms, scheduled for the PRSA Counselors Academy's Spring Conference, is canceled for lack of interest.

APRIL 1993–At two thinly attended Counselors Academy workshops, a Chicago PR firm president explains how she coped with being forced out of her firm's quarters by a natural disaster.

JULY 1993–The biggest flood in the history of Des Moines, IA leaves CMF&Z PR with no running water and most staff members ordered to work from home.

Despite urging clients to prepare for a crisis, most PR firms ignore their own counsel. Few principals have taken the time to develop crisis response and business resumption plans. Have you?

Two types of potential crisis face every PR firm: (1) those that can damage your firm's reputation; and (2) those that can damage your ability to serve your clients.

Here are a few of the potential disasters that can severely damage your firm's reputation: (Thanks to Anne Klein, President, Anne Klein & Associates, Mt. Laurel, NJ, for the list. Reprinted with permission.)

- Accusations, correct or incorrect, by a local, state or U.S. government agency;
- Accusations of poor work by a client;
- Accusations of unethical behavior;
- Agency scandal (discrimination, drugs, sex, etc.);
- Bankruptcy;
- Conflict of interest caused by serving clients in similar fields;
- Conflict of interest caused by moonlighting staffers;

- Controversial clients;
- Controversial firm contribution or pro bono work;
- Controversial statements about the firm's financial stability;
- Controversial statements about the firm's work;
- Controversial statements about the principal or staff;
- Embezzlement;
- Employee diagnosed with AIDS;
- Employee breach of confidentiality;
- Employee misstatement (intentional or otherwise) to a client;
- Employee misstatement (intentional or otherwise) to the public or news media;
- Employee violates noncompete clause;
- Key staffers pitch client, then leave to start own firm;
- Lawsuits (Employee sues agency or vice versa; firm sues client or vice versa; equal opportunity, age discrimination, wrongful discharge or sexual harassment charge filed against agency);
- Abrupt/rapid income drop;
- Layoffs or other high impact/high visibility cost-cutting measures;
- Loss of name partner;
- Serious illness, injury or death of principal;
- Merger (also merger gone sour);
- Misappropriation of ideas (staff member takes ideas/plans/files from another agency or company and gives them to a competing client; staff member takes your ideas/clients to a competing firm);
- SEC, IRS, or other violations of the law;
- Serious media misquote on behalf of firm or client;
- Serious media attack on firm;
- Third party (vendor) nondelivery of services;
- Third party poor performance reflecting on firm either in the eyes of clients or public;
- Unlawful activities on your property; gang fights, drug deals, drug or alcohol use;
- Violation of PRSA Code of Ethics or inquiry by PRSA Judicial Panel.

In addition to legal and reputation problems, you also face potential natural and man-made disasters. What would you do, for example, if your:

- Computer system fails?
- Computer guru quits?
- Key staff member, working on your largest client, quits and/or leaves to work for a client?
- Firm has too much staff turnover in too short a time?
- Staff size is suddenly or drastically reduced and income lost because several of your staff members become pregnant simultaneously?
- Building has a major problem and no one can work inside for several days? (What would you take if you were allowed inside for only a few minutes?)
- Building is damaged/destroyed by fire, destroying all your records?
- Key equipment/documents are stolen?
- Employee is robbed, attacked or killed on or off your property?
- Staff member calls to report he/she has been in an accident en route to a client?
- Staff members and client are in an accident and your insurance lacks adequate liability coverage?
- Employee morale is adversely affected by the loss of one or more key clients?
- Client defaults on a multi-thousand dollar bill?

Here are the types of information that should be in your crisis response/business resumption plan, according to Anne Klein:

- The authorized agency spokesperson(s);
- The person designated to talk with the media, clients, and employees;
- Guidelines for dealing with the news media;
- Guidelines for how to use the fax, copier, phone system and other basic support equipment;

- Guidelines for how the computer system works; where the backup tapes or disks are stored (preferably off-site); how to retrieve them and get the system running again;
- Names, addresses, business/home phone numbers, fax numbers (where appropriate) for all staff members (including a relative's number for emergency use); outside consultants (accountant, attorney, computer programmers, financial planner, insurance broker, management consultant); suppliers (fax, copier, postage meter, telephone service, alternate communication systems); and all key client contacts including home numbers;
- List of banks or financial institutions including account numbers and contracts;
- Location of principal(s) will(s), succession plan, key person and other insurance policies;
- Location of important business documents and financial information kept with third-party consultants;
- Location of off-site storage facility (including name, address, phone, and fax numbers);
- Policy regarding storage/access to central files for client information; and
- Provision for employees to work from home when kept out of the office. (For example, issue each employee a "work at home" kit containing material needed to operate out of the office for at least several days. See below.)

Reprinted with permission of Anne Klein, Anne Klein Associates, Mt. Laurel, NJ.

Here is how two firms handled natural disasters:

When tunnels under Chicago's loop were flooded on a Monday morning, cutting off all electricity in the area, Janet Diederichs & Associates staffers were ordered out of their building on short notice, not to return full time until the following Monday.

Allowed back in the building briefly on Wednesday, each staff member was given a kit of work-at-home materials (every staffer has a computer at home) consisting of additional computer disks, stationery, addresses, phone and fax numbers for clients and the media, and Federal Express and messenger order forms. The firm's answering service was instructed to route calls to Diederichs' apartment.

Said Diederichs, "We didn't lose any business because we were in touch with clients all the time. However, if we hadn't been able to get back into our office briefly, it would probably have been a different story."

While still coping with the flood that largely closed her downtown Des Moines office, Carol Bodensteiner, CMF&Z PR president, said,

> By letting staff members take their computers home (coming into the office only to print copy and send and pick up mail) and communicating with them by E-mail, we're handling most of our clients' ongoing and crisis communication needs. However, we won't know fully what we've missed until we get everyone back in the office.
>
> [Our situation] makes you think; if we couldn't do the work that our clients need, how long would they stay with us? It would have been a lot easier to handle this (the flood) if we'd have thought about it beforehand.

What would you do if your firm was suddenly slapped with an ugly law suit or a fire destroyed your equipment and records? Now is the time to write a crisis plan. Update it regularly; explain it to your staff and dry run it at least annually. Keep copies at your home and those of your senior people as well as in an off-site location such as a bank safety deposit box. Then you'll be as ready as possible when disaster strikes.

PROFILE 17

MIKE WALKER, PRESIDENT, THE WALKER AGENCY, SCOTTSDALE, AZ

Stung by a 1982 corporate "down-sizing," Mike Walker, with wife Mary, jumped into the agency waters. Six weeks later, he had his first client and has been profitable ever since.

The firm's first year's income of about $50,000 has grown to about $1.5 million. Walker provides PR services to outdoor recreation and marine industry clients. He also syndicates a daily three-minute show to 400 radio stations and sends camera-ready material to 10,000 newspapers quarterly.

Asked why they hired his firm, clients said: Creativity, integrity and professional approach. Walker says, "I'm never satisfied, always hungry, always looking for improvement. I never stop learning."

Walker admits that previous agency experience would have been helpful; that he should have broken away earlier from an incompatible partner; should have fired people who needed firing sooner; and should have had "the discipline to make new business a bigger part of my effort."

Starting a firm today, he would minimize hard assets, use hourly rates rather than monthly fees, retain a PR-firm-smart CPA sooner, and spread his clients over more fields.

Advice to principals: "Don't get suckered into debt. Hit the road; nothing beats face time. Make your word your bond. Develop a thick skin and the strongest belief possible in yourself. Understand the power of enthusiasm and use it."

Chapter 17

Fiscal and Physical Checkups

Put it on your calendar now. At least once a quarter, take the time to examine and evaluate your firm's fiscal and physical progress. Look at your numbers. Are you on target to achieve your annual goals? Check your business plan. (What, you don't have one!) Is it working smoothly or missing on one cylinder? Is your firm moving in the right direction?

Here are some guidelines to help you audit your firm's progress four times a year, starting with the end of a year and looking ahead.

END OF YEAR (PROBABLY DECEMBER)

It's a mixed time of the year. Either you are frantically trying to complete assignments so they can be billed in this year's client budgets, or you've used up this year's budgets, or your clients are taking holiday vacations and nothing is happening.

Surveys indicate that three international PR firms–Burson Marsteller, Shandwick, and Hill & Knowlton–do more than half of all the agency business. These and other big international firms will continue to win major, large-budget clients who need multiple offices and/or international capabilities. However, the big firms will continue to be squeezed for profits by cost-conscious clients.

That still leaves lots of good profitable business for the thousands of small- and medium-size firms. Both smaller clients and cost-conscious major clients will continue to look hard at smaller and/or specialized firms to find top-notch service at reasonable, realistic costs. That means good prospects for you (assuming you are not the CEO of a megafirm).

Here are some of the things you should be thinking about to get ready for next year:

- What kind of a year has it been? Did you meet your goals? If not, why not? What did you do right or wrong this year? What is the most important thing to change or begin next year?
- Update your long-range business plan, or write a plan if you do not have one. Then, don't stuff it in a file drawer; follow it.
- Develop a marketing plan and allocate funds to make it work (1 to 3 percent of your income). Commit at least 25 to 40 percent of your own time to new business development.
- Develop and promote a unique strategic position for your firm. Decide what you are or what you want your firm to be, and then let prospects know about it.
- Develop a realistic budget for your firm, based on your best income expectations (see Chapter 13); update and adhere to the budget throughout the year. Change your budget if your income projections change.
- Based on your income expectations, plan staff needs for the next year. Evaluate your staff and get rid of the losers now. If you are in a growth mode, promote or hire a competent senior backup person to run client service while you grow the business.
- Vow to achieve at least an 85 percent productivity average next year. Stop fretting about monthly variances; shoot for long-range results.
- Vow to track client profitability monthly. Know when and why profitability on any account drops below where you want it. And do something about it, even if that means resigning the client. Your firm may be profitable overall, but individual problem clients can pull down total profits.

FIRST QUARTER

Okay, now it's the end of the first quarter. Make sure that you are on track to meet year-end financial goals. Ask yourself these questions:

- Do we have a targeted marketing program? Is it working? Are we making the cold contacts with prospects that everyone hates to make? Are we communicating consistently with prospects? Do we know what makes us different? Do we have a well-conceived strategic position? Are the firm's strategic position and special capabilities well understood by prospects? (See Chapter 4)

- Is our staff in good shape? Do we have the right mix of people to meet unforeseen or likely client needs? Do we have too many, or too few people? Do we have the right balance between junior and senior people to meet our clients' needs and generate a solid profit? Is staff productivity (billable hours) high enough? Are we hanging on to poor performers?
- Are our receivables under control? Do we make weekly calls to clients with bills that are more than 30 days old? Should we stop work for clients whose bills are more than 60 days old? Are we getting advance payments on large out-of-pocket expenses? (Don't be afraid to talk money to clients!)
- Are our expenses on budget and in line with projected income? Are salaries too high as a percent of income? Have we budgeted for salary increases? Is the rent too high? Can we negotiate a lower rate or should we move to cheaper space? Do we need to tighten controls on expenses?
- Will the first quarter be profitable? If not, why not? Do we know the profit returned by each client? Can we turn unprofitable clients around or should we consider resigning them?

SECOND QUARTER

It's nearing the end of your second quarter, but there's still time to improve this year's results. Answer these questions:

- Are productivity, income, expenses and profit in line with projections? If not, why not?
- Are client budgets about half used up? Is there enough money left to do necessary work? Are there any opportunities for new income yet this year?
- Will client budgets hold up? If budget cuts come in the third or fourth quarter, how will we react?

- What are our new business prospects? Are we marketing the firm with discipline and creativity?

THIRD QUARTER

It's fall. The leaves are falling. Are your hopes for the year falling or rising? By now, there is not much you can do to salvage this year. Starting about Thanksgiving, clients and prospects seem to hibernate until they wake up suddenly on January 2nd with new money to spend. Chances are, most client budgets have been spent or committed by now. Hopefully, you'll be able to avoid a late-year budget crimp.

Make sure that all scheduled work can be completed within remaining budgets. You don't want to carry this year's agency time or client budgets over to next year. On the other hand, a client may ask you to bill unused-but-budgeted funds in advance and escrow the money for use next year, so this year's budget will appear used up. Clients sometimes fear budgets will be cut the following year if all the money is not spent in a current year. (An agency vice president of finance, on escrow accounts: "It's a mess, but we do it if the client asks. It's better than losing the money.")

Ask vendors to render invoices in time to be billed to clients this year if the project is in this year's budget. If the project won't actually be finished until early next year, but is in this year's budget, get an advance invoice from the vendor for most of the cost.

Most important, begin planning for next year, if you haven't started already. Client budget sources, particularly product managers (whose current year thinking sometimes stops by August), are probably deep into next year's planning by now. If you want budgets approved for next year, submit proposals early, and start the cycle all over again.

PROFILE 18

JULIE WANG, CEO, WANG HEALTH CARE COMMUNICATIONS, NEW YORK, NY

"A lot of us (entrepreneurs) are basically 'unemployable.' We're not incompetent, just very demanding both of ourselves and the people around us. We're not able or willing to report to people we don't respect. We believe that we can do the job better than anyone else. I've had to work very very hard to overcome that."

This from the chairman of one of the best-known (called "most thoughtful" by *Inside PR*) U.S. health care PR firms; who built her firm from $125,000 in income in 1983 to $3.5 million ten years later. But who started her own agency because she was fired from her job as a national firm vice president.

During the early years of her firm, Wang says she was ". . . too dictatorial, wanted everything done my way; had too high a personal profile; and did not build a team. Then, I was told in no uncertain terms by my staff that if I didn't stop beating up on them and insisting that things be done my way, I would destroy the agency.

"It took me about three years from the time we started the process of empowerment until I finally understood, in my gut, what empowerment meant, what trust meant, and how to make it work both when I needed to intervene and when I needed to lay off and how to negotiate both of those processes."

For new principals, Wang recommends: "Look for the brightest and best (employees) and learn how to lead, nurture and cultivate them."

Chapter 18

And in Conclusion:
New Year's Resolutions

In case you're late coming up with your own this year, or need a bright light to guide you through the night, here are ten New Year's Resolutions designed especially for counseling firm principals. They can be applied at any time during the year. Now is not too soon.

1. I resolve not to lose my head when all around me are losing theirs and when, in reality, all seems lost. Instead, I will step into the hall, blow a mighty blast on the police whistle I keep in my desk for such occasions and yell "Stop the Presses" at the top of my lungs. An account supervisor at Ketchum PR in Pittsburgh used to do just that. Seemed to work fine for her.

2. I resolve to take no more lip than absolutely necessary from crabby clients. Instead, I will subsidize their treatment in an attitude adjustment class. Or, if that fails, I will insist that we do such good work and provide such excellent service to every one of our clients that they will all become sugar-tongued and will no longer beat up on their account executives and other fragile souls.

3. I resolve to be kind to free-lance writers, photographers, artists and all other vendors and suppliers; to always give them careful and complete instructions and plenty of time in which to conclude assignments; and to, always, always pay them promptly (within ten days, if possible).

4. I resolve to hold technology close to my heart and hearth; to spend the bread to buy good networked hardware and sophisticated software that combines time-keeping, accounting, billing, budgeting and profit and productivity tracking and pumps out an information-packed plethora of reports. I will retain one typewriter to ad-

dress an occasional envelope and as a reminder that once upon a time "cut and paste" could not be accomplished with a couple of key strokes.

5. I resolve to pay attention to all the little things that motivate employees and make them eager to come to work. This includes such niceties as: (A) Saying "Thanks," "Great job," and "The client loves you;" (B) Walking the halls frequently with a smile on my lips and a spark in my eyes; (C) Letting people know exactly where they stand through regular candid and comprehensive performance reviews; (D) Not forcing people to ask for a raise, but making sure that everyone knows what our compensation policies are; and (D) Remembering that my replacement may be among my junior staff today.

6. I resolve to challenge and inspire employees by providing the training they need to grow; by suggesting that they become involved in professional organizations and activities; and by encouraging them to climb mountains that they may believe are too steep and treacherous.

7. I resolve to remember that there is life outside the agency business and that people, particularly members of the "X Generation," may not be as fervently devoted to the health and future of this agency as I am.

8. I resolve to remember that not everyone can or will write or perform tasks exactly the way I would, and that this is not necessarily bad. I resolve to delegate both responsibility and authority; and to be patient and learn to tell the difference between an employee approach that is merely different from mine or one that is a threat to the agency.

9. I resolve to encourage people, particularly junior staff members, to have the judgement and confidence in their own ability to stop work on a project before they have invested more time than the client will be willing to pay for.

10. I resolve to remember that good client service is vital to this firm's success. However, for the firm to truly succeed, I must be as good a business executive as I am a public relations counselor.

And in conclusion . . . The words you have just read (I assume that you have just read them. Otherwise, what are you doing way back here?) are the distillation of lessons learned during 25 years in three very good public relations agencies and seven years counseling more than 100 agency principals on a variety of marketing and management problems.

There is really only one more thing that should be said to assure that your time as a public relations firm principal is mightily successful. Have fun! If you've been paying attention, you now know how to run a growing and profitable PR firm. And that's a lot of fun.

APPENDIXES

Appendix A

Sample Time Sheet–
Cawood Communications

Employees of Cawood Communications, Eugene, OR, fill out this paper time sheet daily. Data is then entered into "Project Billing" computer software by the agency bookkeeper.

The "Client" column contains the client name code. The "Number or letters" column contains the client number and project number. The "Code" column contains the code for the type of activity performed. (See the activity codes listed above the sample time sheet.)

"Activity" describes the work specifics. Circled figures in the "T" column and bottom of the page indicate billable time. The printout shows total costs by client with a subtotal by individual job numbers.

The printout also shows employee billable hour totals.

	19 Art Direction	26 Copywriting	33 Interview	40 Research			
NAME:_____	20 Bidding	27 Creative	34 Media Buying	41 Review			
DATE:_____	21 Calls	28 Delivery	35 Media Planning	42 Supervise			
Unbillable Codes. Admin. (A)	22 Clerical	29 Design	36 Meeting	43 Touring			
Client Rel. (CR) Float Day (FD)	23 Computer Prod.	30 Editing	37 Planning	44 Travel			
New Client Dev. (NCD)	24 Consulting	31 File/Organize	38 Preparation	45 Vendor Coordin.			
Organizations (O) Personal (P)	25 Coordination	32 Illustration	39 Proofing	46 Broadcast			
Pro Bono (PB) Personal/Medical				Direction/Prod.			
(PM) Sick (S) Training (T)							
Vacation (V)							

TIME	CLIENT	Number or Letter	CODE	ACTIVITY	NC	T	THINGS TO DO
7:30							SUB review materials/estimates
7:45							EO minutes
8:00	SUB	22-201	26	Write Newspaper Ad			Andrea re: table tents
8:15							CPOF Radio Ad
8:30						10	HH Edits
8:45		↓					Buell November Ad Buy
9:00	EO	245-003	36	In-House Planning			Set up Mtg—Jim
9:15				Meeting			Solar Ad to Cornelia
9:30							
9:45							
10:00						20	
10:15							
10:30							
10:45		↓					
11:00		A	31				
11:15							
11:30	CPOF	276-002	21	Ed Howard		5	
11:45	WEYER	93-002	21	Jane Smith		15	
12:00		LUNCH					
12:15							
12:30							
12:45		↓					
1:00	CPOF	276-011	25	New Projects to Dave	✓		
1:15	EWEB	61-071	37			15	
1:30							
1:45							
2:00	SUB	22-203	41	List		15	
2:15		A	25	Read PR Magazine			
2:30		↓	21				
2:45		NCD	21	CAMAX — Jan Brown			
3:00	NCK W	246-002	36	SH—JC Ad		15	PHONE CALLS TO MAKE
3:15							John M 689-7331
3:30		↓					Dave Plummer — R&R
3:45		O	44				Jeff — Rectsport
4:00			36	Chamber of Commerce			Donna
4:15				Board Mtg			
4:30							
4:45							
5:00							
5:15							
5:30		↓	44				
5:45							
6:00							
6:15							
6:30							
6:45				5.25			
7:00							

Appendix B

Sample Computer Time Sheet–
Phase Two Strategies

This on-line computer time-keeping system is used by employees of Phase Two Strategies, San Francisco. Employees enter time directly into their computer. TimeSlips software programs are available in DOS, Windows, and McIntosh versions.

The computer software prompts staff member to enter name, client, type of activity, billable or nonbillable time and a description of the activity. The activity description automatically scrolls to provide additional space.

In the printout, the cost is automatically calculated using the employee's hourly rate from the data base. Client reports and invoices can be generated from billable time data.

Sample Screen from TimeSlips III

TSTimerApp

Slip 1189 of 1248 | ACTIVE | -4 active slips
Slip Value $ 160.23

| Mini View |
| Turn off |
| Delete |
| Report |
| Help |

Found:0

Professional | SBR S Rozmanith

Activity | Prof Services

Client | UW—United Way

Project | 1. Marketing Counsel

What Works publicity efforts ——
• Reviewed mesage Ed left about notable
people in each county
• Called Joe Haraburda, Oakland Tribune —
left message to follow up— he had

○ 95.00
○ 0.00
○ 30.00
○ Fixed value

● Billable
○ Unbillable
○ No Charge
○ Hold
○ Summary

Time Estimated 0:00:00

Date 11/1/94
thru 11/1/94

Time 8:49 AM   Spent 1:41:12

☐ Recurring   ☐ Add to Flat Fee

229

Appendix C

Monthly Status Report–
Jack Guthrie & Associates

A continuous flow of information from agency to client not only informs the client of the agency's work in his behalf, but also confirms instructions and decisions.

Monthly status reports (only first pages of reports shown) used by Jack Guthrie & Associates, Louisville, KY describe the progress and status of the agency's assignments on behalf of clients over the past month. Reports such as these should accompany invoices or follow quickly after. Other important reports should cover meetings and media contacts.

A good flow of agency reports helps merchandise the agency's accomplishments and emphasizes account stewardship.

JACK GUTHRIE & ASSOCIATES, INC.
Public Relations
710 West Main Street
Louisville, Kentucky 40202-2676
(502) 584-0371
Telefax 502/584-0207

To: Judi Ryce
From: Dan Hartlage
Subject: Invoice, Summary of Activities for October 1994

Date: November 14, 1994
Client: William M. Mercer
Copies: Jack Guthrie
Mike Gross

The following activities have been carried out by Jack Guthrie & Associates, Inc. on behalf of William M. Mercer, Inc. during October 1994:

GENERAL SERVICES (3465-01)

- Internal client team meetings regarding Nashville media opportunities, potential development of feature column by Dr. Schanie for placement in key business publications.

- Frequent telephone correspondences with J. Ryce, T. Tyler, S. Sharp, J. Adkins regarding Nashville media opportunities, development of news release on 1994 Greater Louisville Area Wage Survey, securing telephone number and telephone book listing for Nashville market, and general discussions on upcoming activities.

- Meeting (10/10) with T. Tyler, J. Ryce regarding various upcoming activities and opportunities, including editorial calendars for Louisville and Nashville business weeklies, seminar schedule through January 1995, and logistics of obtaining a Nashville-based telephone number.

- Frequent telephone conversations with South Central Bell, Yellow Page representatives regarding logistics/options of obtaining Nashville telephone number.

- Frequent telephone conversations with Nashville business media regarding Mercer's upcoming seminar activities; conversations with Louisville and Nashville media regarding editorial calendars for 1994-95.

- General client services, including monitoring of local media, development of summary for September 1994 activities.

- Provided all necessary account, clerical/administrative support for correspondences, reports, mailings, etc.

Reprinted with permission of Richard Mayes, President, Jack Guthrie & Associates, Inc.

JACK GUTHRIE & ASSOCIATES, INC.
Public Relations
710 West Main Street
Louisville, Kentucky 40202-2676
(502) 584-0371
Telefax 502/584-0207

To:	Ed O'Daniel	Date:	October 29, 1993
From:	Dan Hartlage	Client:	Kentucky Distillers
Subject:	Summary of Activities	Copies:	Rick Mayes
	for September 1993		Mike Gross

The following activities were carried out by Jack Guthrie & Associates, Inc. during the month of September 1993, on behalf of Kentucky Distillers Association in support of the 1993 Bourbon Export Program:

OVERSEAS PARTNER AGENCY MANAGEMENT

* Internal discussions, review of overseas media relations activities and progress of public relations partners in Greece, Thailand and Taiwan. Correspondence with public relations partners regarding monitoring media placement of stories related to Kentucky tours and Bourbon tastings, and discussions with partners regarding all aspects of overseas program.

CREATIVE SERVICES

* Ongoing telephone and written correspondence with E. O'Daniel and Maker's Mark representatives regarding all aspects of Bourbon tastings scheduled for September 27 (Taiwan) and September 28 (Thailand). Correspondence included development of tasting agenda, complete travel itinerary, all details related to the tasting event.

Also, ongoing correspondence with public relations partners in Thailand and Taiwan, as well as with representatives from the U.S. Embassy in Thailand and the American Institute in Taiwan, regarding tasting events. Correspondence focused on all aspects related to the tastings—overall format and agenda, availability of all Bourbon brands and other food and beverage items, hotel accommodations for KDA representatives, invitation list, media interest/ availability, etc.

Reprinted with permission of Richard Mayes, President, Jack Guthrie & Associates, Inc.

JACK GUTHRIE & ASSOCIATES, INC.
Public Relations
710 West Main Street
Louisville, Kentucky 40202-2676
(502) 584-0371
Telefax 502/584-0207

To: Barbara McDaniel
From: Mike Gross
Subject: Summary of Activities for July 1994

Date: August 9, 1994
Client: Toyota Motor Manufacturing
Copies: Jim Wiseman
Jack Guthrie
Rick Mayes
Clair Nichols

The following activities were carried out by Jack Guthrie & Associates on behalf of Toyota Motor Manufacturing, U.S.A., Inc. during the month of July 1994:

GENERAL CLIENT SERVICE/ACCOUNT SUPERVISION (4800-01)

- Overall coordination of account planning and implementation; internal account team meetings to monitor progress on all projects; briefings with client to update on status of projects; review of background materials supplied by client.

CLERICAL SUPPORT (4800-02)

- All clerical activities for all projects, including typing, proofing, copying, faxing and coordination of delivery services.

SPECIAL PROJECTS (4800-03)

- Began researching means for handling visitors center tour reservations.

J.D. POWER (4800-04)

- All phases of planning and implementation of J. D. Power plant event, including: scripting and production of team member video; event agenda development; coordination with Bruce Jenner; preparation and distribution of media advisories and releases and made follow-up calls; day-of-coordination of event and Jenner's appearance.

Reprinted with permission of Richard Mayes, President, Jack Guthrie & Associates, Inc.

Appendix D

Computer Budgeting Form–
The Benjamin Group

This on-line computer form is used by The Benjamin Group, Campbell, CA to prepare client budgets. The firm is developing on-line historical data of past client work as a budgeting resource.

The program uses Windows Excel spreadsheet. Staff members enter estimated time required by various employees to complete different aspects of the project. The activity list on the left of the form is standard depending on type of project being budgeted.

The printout automatically calculates the total cost using employees' hourly rates in the data base. (The hourly rates shown are out of date.) The program provides a common starting point for budget development, ensures a standard, disciplined approach to the budgeting process and reminds practitioners of factors to be included in the budget.

Cost estimate serves as the basis for the "Project Authorization Form" that the client approves. Itemized data are not shown to the client.

Client: UNICODE INC.
Project: New Members News Release
Job #: 66-1003
Date: March 13, 1991

Enter Hours:	Cler	AC	AR	AE	SAE	AS	MS	Dir/GM	Princ
Planning									
Research/Read									
Client Mtgs									
Travel									
Estimating					0.25				
Correspon									
Vendor Mtgs									
Proj Coord		0.50							
Writing					5.00				
Proofing									
Editing					1.00	1.00			0.50
Edit Calls									
Edit Corres									
Edit Meet									
Gen Acct Mgmt									
Team Mtgs									
Acct Coord									
Acct Superv					0.50	0.50			
other									
other									
other									

	Hours	Rate	Total	Initials
Clerical	0.00	25.00	0.00	————
AC	0.50	50.00	25.00	————
AR	0.00	75.00	0.00	————
AE	0.00	90.00	0.00	————
SAE	6.75	100.00	675.00	————
AS	1.50	115.00	172.50	————
MS	0.00	125.00	0.00	————
Dir/GM	0.00	140.00	0.00	————
Princ	0.50	175.00	87.50	————
Total PR	9.25		960.00	

Buyouts Included?

Source: Steve Benjamin, Principal, The Benjamin Group. Reprinted with permission.

Index

Page numbers followed by "f" indicate Figures.